PATRICK
DUFFY

PATRICK DUFFY

The Man Behind Bobby Ewing

Lee Riley

W.H. ALLEN · LONDON
1987

Copyright © Lee Riley, 1987

Typeset in Concorde Roman by Phoenix Photosetting
Printed and bound in Great Britain by
Mackays of Chatham Ltd, Chatham, Kent
for the Publishers, W.H. Allen & Co. Plc
44 Hill Street, London W1X 8LB

ISBN 0 491 03246 3

This Book Is Dedicated To The Memory Of
TERRENCE AND MARIE DUFFY

CONTENTS

ACKNOWLEDGEMENTS

This book is a result of the combined efforts and co-operation of many people. The author would like to express her gratitude to:

Mary Toledo, Dan Yakir, Tom Green and Judy Kirby, for their excellent editorial and research assistance;

Art editor Amanda Rubin, St. Martin's Press editors Tom Dunne, Laura Jack and Betsy Williams, and 2M Communications' Madeleine Morel, Karen Moline and Kelly Leisten, for turning ideas into print;

Colleagues Tony Brenna, Sam Rubin, Rick Taylor, Steve Devitt, Ian Marquand, Russell Turiak, Craig Modderno, Greg Hoffman, Joe Policy and Phil Ramey, for their expertise and insights;

All those who graciously sat still for interviews – Arnie Zaslove, Bill Eaton, Chuck Varga, Diane Newberry, Deborah Presley, Rick Bloom, and a few whose names will never see print;

John Hunt, whose support and advice were invaluable;

And, as always, Russell Alexander.

'The difference between fact and fiction is that fiction is about life. None of you will ever be as real to me as is Anna Karenina.'

– O'Henry Award-winning author
Dr. Marvin Mudrick, to his students.

INTRODUCTION

More than a hundred million Americans have spent Friday evenings with Patrick Duffy – or, at any rate, with his alter ego Bobby Ewing. There are half a *billion* people around the world who consider him a personal friend. *Dallas* regulars probably know more intimate details about the Ewing family than they do about their own blood relatives.

Over the past ten years, we have watched Bobby Ewing mature from a self-indulgent playboy into a business giant. We rooted for him when he defied a family feud to marry his Juliet, Pam Barnes. We supported him in his ongoing opposition to big bad brother J.R. We wept with him time and again when Pam lost their baby. We gasped when Bobby was kidnapped, blinded . . . and ultimately, killed.

The 'death' of Bobby Ewing unleashed a furor among television audiences unprecedented in the medium's history. Not since Sherlock Holmes tumbled over the Reichenbach Falls has the public so vociferously demanded a dramatic retraction. *Dallas* producers bowed to the pressure; Bobby was brought back to life in the most controversial prime-time plot twist ever devised.

True, Bobby Ewing is an awfully nice guy. Moral, loving, patient, good-hearted, well-intentioned. You could almost describe him as Christ-like. Still, resurrection is going a bit far – even for a soap opera. Yet, on 26 September 1986, sixty million TV sets showed Bobby Ewing come back from the dead.

Thanks to the self-perpetuating cycle of celebrity created by today's mass communications, Patrick Duffy's personal life became increasingly newsworthy as interest in *Dallas* skyrocketed. To viewers in ninety-eight countries around the world, the personal life of Patrick Duffy was officially public property.

Unfortunately for the popular press, Duffy was never good tabloid fodder. A private, unostentatious man, he didn't partake of the Hollywood highlife. Happily married for the past 15 years to ballerina Carlyn Rosser, Patrick lives in slow-lane suburbia; the family occupies the same house today that they bought for $170,000 in 1978. (If that sounds expensive by non-California standards, remind yourself that other stars spend as much for a car!) The Duffy sons, Padraic and Connor, have never grabbed headlines for drug busts or nightclub hijinks. Of course, they're still in primary school, but they're also well-behaved. The only time Connor earned a gossip page write-up was when the family dog bit him – a story that actually made Page One in London!

That half a dozen reporters were calling a hospital emergency room for the gory details about a puncture wound eventually treated with a tetanus shot and a sticking plaster exemplifies the enormous curiosity surrounding the man behind Bobby. Duffy has often said that Bobby Ewing is about 80% Patrick Duffy – that the actor moulds the character and puts much of himself into this larger-than-life Texan. But what part of Patrick Duffy is in Bobby Ewing – and why is that ingredient so vital that a blockbuster television series should sink ten places on the Neilsen rating chart without it?

Bobby Ewing was born in Texas in 1948, doted on by his fabulously wealthly parents and raised with a love of the land and an inner strength that has served him well through his life. Patrick Duffy was born in Montana in 1949, doted on by his dirt-poor parents and raised with a love of the land and an inner strength that has also served him well through his life.

Bobby and Patrick were both outstanding high school athletes – although Patrick gave up football for drama class while Bobby went on to become a star quarterback on his university team. Each played the field, too, when it came to the ladies – until that one inevitable woman stopped him in his tracks. For both Patrick and his character, though for different reasons, the fated mate was considered by family and friends totally unthinkable. And while Bobby divorced and remarried his Pam (and, depending on scriptwriters' whims, may soon replace her altogether), Patrick Duffy has cleaved unto Carlyn with a devotion that some call obsessive.

From 2 April 1978 (the day Bobby Ewing first graced a TV screen) until 16 May 1986 (when the late Bobby

Ewing materialized in his widow's shower), 'Bobby' and 'Patrick' dutifully kept their distinct places in the scheme of things. Fact was fact, and fiction was fiction, and never the twain need meet. If *Dallas* fans were simultaneously interested in the dramatic doings of the Ewings, as well as intrigued by the private lives of its cast, at least they didn't confuse the two. When Bobby rejoined *Dallas*, the lines suddenly started to blur. Somehow, the person was no longer distinct from the persona; Bobby and Patrick were magically merged.

Over the years we became accustomed to watching Bobby Ewing save the day on *Dallas*; now, it was *Patrick Duffy* coming to save the day FOR *Dallas*. Headlines promising the 'untold story' of Bobby and Jenna's love child were displayed alongside headlines revealing the 'untold story' of Patrick's devotion to Buddhism. Which is more 'real'? Patrick Duffy's salary? Or the net worth of Ewing Oil? Each, certainly, was equally newsworthy.

Then fate dealt the flesh-and-blood Patrick Duffy a blow no scriptwriter would dare inflict on a beloved character: Only weeks after Bobby came back to life, Patrick's own parents were horribly killed. Not 'killed off,' like Kristin or Digger or so many others. Really killed, with real bullets. Real blood. No amount of fan mail could turn their deaths into a bad dream; no network executive could order Terrence and Marie Duffy back to the set. On 18 November 1986 life imitated soap opera – and it wasn't fun any more.

It's an unhappy irony that this armed robbery at a rural tavern would have passed with no more than a paragraph's notice if the victims' son were someone else. 'Montana Couple Killed In Hold-Up,' sadly, isn't international news; 'Patrick Duffy's Parents Murdered' is. The drunken teenagers since convicted of the crime had no idea they were killing a star's mum and dad; they only wanted a handful of crumpled bills from the cash register.

And while it seemed – indeed, was – a ghoulish media circus that descended on Boulder, Montana, it was also an unavoidable one. Millions of caring, worried 'friends' of Bobby/Patrick sincerely wanted to know exactly what they'd want to know if the tragedy had happened to their own neighbours: 'How did it happen? Who did it? Have they caught them? Is there anything I can do to help?'

The only way to answer those questions for half the world at once was to assign hardened journalists from around the globe to that one-stoplight town. And a long-standing, delicately symbiotic relationship between celebrity and celebrity press turned parasitic; 'Who Shot The Duffys?' was given the same handling as 'Who Shot J.R.?' It was just another juicy plot twist; journalists who would habitually badger, beg or bribe *Dallas* insiders for cliffhanger clues were using identical techniques on Duffy kin. Childhood photos commanded the same cash bounty as Xeroxed scripts.

Patrick Duffy had always wanted to be famous. But he never wanted to be a one-man mini-series. The saddest irony of all is that this tragic loss gave Patrick Duffy 'household name' status far and away above what he had earned before. Had he known what the price was going to be, would he ever have paid?

In the final analysis, who is Patrick Duffy? Underneath all the sensationalism is a real person, a breathing being with thoughts and emotions much deeper than the two-dimensional character we see on the printed page or TV screen.

Patrick Duffy is a complex man, full of contradictions. He's a skilled Shakespearean actor – who happily does television commercials. He's devoted to his wife, ten years older than he – but told 20 million television viewers that he had cheated on her. He is committed to his Buddhist faith and a respected leader of his temple – but he only adopted the religion to impress a date. His greatest natural talent, according to his acting teachers, is his comedic ability – yet he has played exactly one comic role in his professional career. He's an astute businessman who has methodically amassed millions – and he contentedly drives around in a seven-year-old Jeep.

He's outspoken, unconventional, unpredictable and, according to those near him, as goodhearted as Bobby Ewing himself.

You've known Bobby for ten years. Now meet Patrick Duffy.

1

Growing Up Country

If you're a good Irish Catholic named Terrence, and your wife is a good Irish Catholic named Marie, and she gives birth to your son on the morning of 17 March, you have few choices about what to call him. So on St Patrick's Day of 1949, it was Patrick Duffy – strapping, healthy and yowling – who came head first into the world. His mother, Marie – 'Babe' to her friends – was 26; daddy Terrence – known to all as 'Duff' – was 29. Patrick was their second child, their first son, and destined to be the only son and baby of the family forever. Big sister Joanne accepted this new competition with all the equanimity one could expect of a three-year-old.

There were about 600 full-time residents in the community of Townsend, Montana, when Patrick made his debut. (Today, the population has climbed to a staggering 1,587.) It was mainly a farming and mining town – although most of the mines closed down by the early Fifties. Hunting and fishing were the recreational mainstays: 'It's sort of like Norman Rockwell's paintings brought to life,' said Patrick.

[17]

Baby Patrick was doted on by a large and close-knit family; his aunts and uncles alone numbered 10. But Terrence Duffy, a strong-willed and physically strong man's man, soon left the cozily rural nest to seek adventure and fortune in harsher climes. Patrick was three when the Duffys packed up and set out for Alaska.

Fortune didn't make itself apparent. 'We lived on the eight dozen eggs we brought with us,' Duffy once joked. Terrence looked unsuccessfully for work as a carpenter, and 'played cribbage,' as Patrick recalled. After two years, the family moved back to Montana.

This time, they settled in the community of Boulder, about 20 miles east of their old home, Townsend, and 30 miles south of the state capital, Helena. In 1955, Terrence and Marie bought a quiet tavern called The Owl, which they later renamed The Lounge. Although they leased the place out to other operators at various times in their lives, they owned the Lounge until the day they died – behind its own polished bar, on 18 November 1986.

There's one traffic light in Boulder, and a main drag (called, of course, Main Street) that boasts a hardware store, a post office, two grocery stores, a motel, a restaurant and five saloons. Snuggled in Boulder Valley, the town borders the Elkhorn range, and is a jumping-off point for deer and elk hunting in season. It's hospitable yet clannish, proud of its rugged individualists, and totally unenamoured of Hollywood glamour and glitz.

'It's easy growing up in Montana,' Patrick said. 'There aren't a lot of obstacles. Fishing in the summer.

Sledding in the winter. Loving parents. And my dog, Blue,' he laughed. Childhood pal Ron Zendron said he and Patrick were Tom Sawyer and Huckleberry Finn come to life: chasing after snakes, angling for trout, trampling paths through virgin meadows.

All this sweetness and light, though, had a flip side. For one thing, there was no money. 'We were exceptionally poor,' is how Patrick flatly described it. Racing through meadows barefoot makes a wonderful memory picture, but rare is the kid who wouldn't just as soon have a dirt bike, thanks. The family living quarters where Patrick and Joanne Duffy were raised consisted of a two-bedroom apartment at the back of the bar. Joanne recalled many a time when some patron would stumble into the family kitchen, thinking he was pointed toward the men's room. She became adept at gently heading confused (and unzipped) customers back in the right direction. On Sundays, when the bar was closed by virtue of Montana's Blue Laws, the tavern became the Duffy kids' playpen.

'Gowing up in a tavern wasn't a bad thing,' Patrick once said. 'It was really kind of an adventure, and we were very independent and self-reliant children.' And if the tavern never made the family well-to-do – this was, after all, a solidly working-class establishment; in 1986, a draught beer at the Lounge still cost only 75 cents – it certainly kept them from starving. True, at times their dinner entree was lentil beans, but in general they were comfortable enough, and happy. There was a lot of hard work – Terrence and Marie tended the bar themselves from 10 a.m. to 2 a.m., six days a week, with Babe generally taking day shift and Duff the evenings – but there was also a lot of love there.

'I looked up to my father a lot,' said Patrick. 'He was very handsome, always the centre of attention. He ruled the roost. I wanted to be just like him.' Marie Duffy remembered that 'Patrick told everyone he wanted to be a bartender when he grew up.'

Terrence and Patrick went hunting and fishing together. Patrick rode in a rodeo when he was 10. He played Little League baseball. He earned pocket money doing chores after school on a neighbouring ranch. Ronald Reagan would have wept with joy at the sight of the Duffy family scrapbook; this was a revisionist's Utopia, and Patrick the perfect poster boy for the Republican Party's version of the American Dream. Except for the difference of vast wealth, Patrick Duffy's childhood was not unlike Bobby Ewing's. The values instilled, certainly, were similar: love and respect for parents, self-reliance, independence, rugged individualism in a harsh environment, an affinity for nature, a sense of discipline. These are hardly negative qualities. If there's one word to categorically describe Patrick Duffy's early years, it's one that Duffy himself has often used: 'old-fashioned.'

It was certainly not an upbringing one would expect to produce a Buddhist actor who runs away with a married dancer 10 years his senior.

Patrick's fourth grade teacher remembers him as 'bright, serious and quiet.' His mum called him 'clever, thoughtful, caring and naturally funny.'

Years before he could verbalize his desire to be the centre of attention – just like his dad – Patrick exhibited a tendency to command the spotlight. 'Pat was a real beer-lover as a baby,' Terrence once said in a rare, and widely reprinted interview. 'He just loved to drain the cans.' This, naturally, drew amused appreciation from onlookers. Once, when he was about a decade shy of the drinking age, Patrick went with his family to a local wedding, and he and his little friends managed to reach past the fruit drink and guzzle from the grown-ups' spiked punchbowl instead. 'By the time we discovered it, the little guy was completely smashed!' laughed Terrence.

Although some published reports have it that Duffy today is a teetotaller because of those early, overambitious experiments with booze, Duffy says that such isn't the case. 'I drink with the best o' them,' confides the actor with a stereotypical Irish twinkle. 'I don't find drinking silly. I get silly from drinking!'

'Duffy – The Early Years' would have made a good chapter in Garrison Keillor's *Prairie Home Companion*, if not in itself a prime-time screenplay: Tragedy! At age eight, he suffered a bout of rheumatic fever, serious enough that Marie had fears for her son's life. Hijinks! When he was 10, he was playing 'chicken' with a bow and arrow – and shot his best friend in the leg. 'He didn't do it on purpose,' recalled the unintended target, John Paradis. 'He was just lousy with a bow!' Thrills! Patrick jumped onto haystacks from barn rooftops, and walked the 50-foot-high gutters of the courthouse building to prove his moxie. Spills! He borrowed the family pick-up truck for a joyride, and promptly ran it into a ditch.

The senior Duffy's concept of discipline was to have

the kids – equal treatment for Patrick and Joanne alike – bend over, to grab their ankles and give them a whack on the rear with a flyswatter. 'It never really hurt,' said Patrick. 'It was sort of an embarrassment.'

When Patrick was 13, the family moved again – and the nascent teen got a new outlook on life. The Seattle suburb of Everett, Washington isn't exactly a booming metropolis, but it's a far cry from Boulder. 'Whoa!' said Duffy. 'There's a lot more to life than I thought!'

At Olympic View Junior High, Patrick Duffy broke through the shell of his rural isolation. He ran for class office (and won). He got involved in the school's sports teams: track, pole-vaulting, football. (Tall as he was, Patrick said 'I was never any good at basketball.') He participated in a rather adolescent class play – a Western, wouldn't you know it, called 'He Tried With His Boots On.'

At Cascade High School, he was a star player on the football team up until his junior year. When he quit the team itself ('I didn't like getting hurt!') he was elected team cheerleader. He became class clown. He joined the Drama Club. He got certified as a scuba diver in the Puget Sound (taking free lessons from Joanne, who was studying to become an oceanographer – lessons which would come in very handy for his big television break.) He made the Honor Society (although his grades would later drop back to the mid-B's). And he discovered girls (which might explain those B's!)

'Girls *smell* better than locker rooms,' he told his mum. Tall, dark-haired, hazel-eyed – maybe a bit skinny – Patrick found his appreciation of womankind returned in kind . . . eventually. Former schoolmates have reported, with a smirk, that Patrick's early dating efforts were singularly unsuccessful. Somewhere out there, an unknown number of Cascade High alumnae could just *kick* themselves for having said no.

As his high school career progressed, Patrick toyed with the idea of becoming either an architect or a professional athlete. He became popular – in part, said one female former schoolmate, because 'he wasn't so full of himself.' Neither 'sissy' nor 'macho,' the tee-naged Duffy had 'an easy self-confidence that so many other boys seemed to lack'. A male ex-classmate remembered him as 'really good to talk to. He always made you feel that he was really interested in what you were saying.' Marie used to say that Patrick was the kind of kid who 'would play ball with the kids that no one else played with – while still keeping his regular friends.'

Patrick worked part-time to buy himself the little luxuries of life – like clothes. Again, the family was only barely making ends meet. Patrick and Terrence, in fact, had done the bulk of construction work on the family home with their own hands. Patrick took a part-time job as a mechanic, another as a garage attendant. He sold shoes at J. C. Penney. Then one day he was told that there was a way of making money doing the single thing he had come to love above all other things. No, not making out with girls. Acting. And for Patrick Duffy, All-American Boy, everything changed.

2

Shifting Gears

'I was bent on becoming an architect,' Duffy once told journalist Tom Jory, 'and was aiming in that direction in high school.' But, as Patrick notes in his official talent agency biography, 'high school dramatics changed all that.

'I found that I *liked* being out in front of all those people,' he reminisced in a 1977 interview. 'I liked the atmosphere. That plus the encouragement I got from my drama teacher led to my decision to go into theatre.'

Junior high teacher Harriet Shore was the first to involve Patrick in class plays, and feels that 'even then, he wanted to entertain people.' But it was a few years later that the teenager became serious about the idea.

'In high school, I had an instructor in the drama department named Maxine Dysart. She was the first person to tell me that actors are actually paid for their efforts! She encouraged my potential by investigating the Professional Actors Training Programme at the University of Washington. Over 1200 actors auditioned for the programme, and I was one of 12 selected.

[25]

'It was the first professional trade school for actors. Our time was utilized strictly for acting projects. Unlike Drama majors, who had foreign language requirements or costume design or make-up courses, all we did was act – or study things which would directly relate to onstage preparation.' The course included everything from Medieval passion plays to mime – with an emphasis on Shakespeare. It was the brainchild of Arnie Zaslove – now a director at the Bath House Theatre in Washington – and the late Duncan Ross, who succeeded John Houseman as head of the University of Southern California's theatre arts department.

'I first taught Patrick in the 1967-68 term,' recalls Zaslove. 'We had just instituted the professional training programme; I was the first teacher there, in fact.

'The talent level in the programme was very high. Patrick didn't really stand out that much at the time, to be honest, because the calibre of the students altogether was so extraordinary. He stayed with us for three years, taking a full line of roles in classical theatre.

'My impressions? He was very talented. He was a very good comedian, very physical. A natural acrobat. He was . . . facile. At the time, I even said he was *too* facile. I felt he was trying to perform too much. I told him, "You can just go down to Hollywood now and probably get work, or you can invest three years of your life and develop yourself a little deeper than simply doing the things that come easily to you."

'He stayed.'

Interestingly, Zaslove saw in Patrick first and fore-most an incipient comedian, an uncostumed clown. Duffy was an athlete, a highly physical performer whose quick wit and muscular fitness were his most obvious attributes. 'I cast him in a lot of roles that required physical things,' says Zaslove. 'I used him in the children's theatre a lot. That clowning ability – which is very rare – stayed with him. I'm surprised, frankly, that it's the one thing he doesn't seem to have done in his professional career. He was a natural.

'I always felt that, at the time, Patrick still wasn't exactly sure what he wanted to do with his life.'

He might not yet have determined what it was he wanted to do with the rest of his life, but the rigours of an acting career certainly took up every minute of life as he knew it. Duffy told writer David Houston: 'For four years, I was in this constant regime from 9 in the morning to 4 in the afternoon – fencing, juggling, speech training, circus technique, singing, combat . . . anything that involved acting.' Instructors included mimes imported from France, gymnasts from the Olympic team, and members of the Barnum and Bailey circus. 'After class, in the evening, we either performed or rehearsed for the next play. In the summers, we were hired to do summer seasons of about five plays plus two children's shows.'

And in between all this, Patrick would drive 20 miles each night to his part-time job as a hospital janitor. 'I'm not sure I ever slept at all,' he once joked. But it turned out not to be a very funny joke after all.

It was during his senior year that he developed what started out as a mild – and well-earned – case of laryngitis. Ignoring (of course) doctor's warnings to rest his vocal chords, he continued his exhausting schedule unabated. 'I was working in two plays, going to school, and singing in a production with the Seattle Opera Company. It was,' he admitted in retrospect, 'very foolish on my part.'

Patrick ruptured his larynx. 'Slowly the blood vessels started erupting,' Patrick recalled with a shiver. 'One day, it all went *ka-phhutt*, and everything broke.'

This time, the doctors' warnings could not be ignored. A specialist was consulted; the options were dismal. Patrick could submit to dangerous surgery – surgery that offered no guarantee of a cure – or he could shut up, not say a single solitary word, for whatever period of time it might take to heal the vocal chords. It was that, or be mute forever. 'I graduated without a voice,' said Duffy.

For two months, he lived in total silence. He communicated by writing notes; on the phone, he whistled to let callers know a human person was on the line, and then handed the instrument over to someone else.

The talented, hearing-impaired actress Marlee Matlin may have won the Academy Award in 1987 for her role as a deaf-mute in *Children of a Lesser God*, but in general, lack of a voice is hardly an asset for an aspiring thespian. Patrick Duffy was terrified. But he was also resourceful. Upon graduation, he worked within the system to find a niche where he could mark time – and not abandon his chosen career. With the help and advice of a staff reporter from the *Seattle Times*, Patrick negotiated with the state administration to create the position of Washington's appointed 'actor in residence' – and promptly filled it himself.

What he mainly did was teach government-funded classes in mime and movement (neither of which, conveniently, required a whole lot of talking) and, after he began to heal, narrate for the performances of visiting theatrical troupes – opera, symphony orchestras and (mark this one well) ballet companies. 'I was able to speak very, very softly,' he recalled, 'and depend upon a microphone for amplification. It was torture, but I got through it.'

In 1971, Patrick was teaching mime to high school students, and leading tension-relieving body movement classes for other actors. Then he was called to narrate a performance by a New York-based ballet troupe on tour through Washington, the First Chamber Dance Company. 'I was in pig heaven,' Patrick recalled, when he took his first look at the line-up of ballerinas. 'There were five dancers in the company, and I thought "Great! I'll work my way through them, starting on the left."

'Carlyn was first on the left.'

And the day Patrick Duffy met Carlyn Rosser, the young buck stopped here.

3

New Directions

Seattle, 1971, Patrick Duffy is 22 years old, 6′ 2″ tall and weighs in at a little under 12 stone. He's long, lean and lithe, an athlete and a cut-up. His mane of dark brown curls shines almost like ebony in the sun. Those big eyes glisten gold to green to smokey grey when he turns them on you; his cheekbones could give you a papercut. Is it any wonder that once shy Patrick – who steady-dated only one girl through his final years of high school – should go from playing Romeo to becoming one?

'I love women,' said Duffy. 'All shapes and sizes. It's one of my great vices. I am probably attracted to more women than any man has a right to be.'

Patrick freely admitted that he fooled around like a randy rabbit in his college days. 'I never stayed with anyone long enough to get comfortable,' though, he told reporter Mary Murphy. And then he met Carlyn Rosser.

'At first, I was attracted to her because of the way she looked in leotards,' he said. And Carlyn was something to see: icy blonde, with porcelain skin and the eyes of a

Keene painting. A ballerina since she was 15 years old, she had legs that seemed to start somewhere around her collarbone. Patrick was smitten.

There were only two problems. One, Carlyn was ten years older than Patrick. Two, she was already married.

And, of course, Patrick was at this point still communicating in a less-than-sexy hoarse whisper – or with a notepad and pencil. Recalled Carlyn, 'I thought he was boring.'

'She didn't even like me,' Duffy told Barbara Walters. 'I really had to work on her. I was just a schoolkid, and she was a married woman.'

Patrick wrote cute notes to his lady love, and attached them to bouquets of flowers – at least, that's how the romance was described in the Sunday supplement to Britain's *News of the World* . . . a tabloid without a 50% accuracy ratio.

Patrick pursued; Carlyn rebuffed. He told her, 'I prefer older women!' Nothing swayed her, until one day he asked the indefatigable dancer to what she attributed her boundless energy and stamina. It was, he later admitted, only a ploy – a good come-on line. And yet it was the one line that, finally, worked. Carlyn answered his question and, in doing so, opened up to him for the first time.

'I had come back from a long trip,' Carlyn told *People* magazine in 1985. 'I walked right into rehearsal and started working really hard and he said, "How do you do that?" And I told him that I chanted the words *nam-myoho-renge-kyo*, and introduced him to Buddhism, and eventually our love came out of that.'

The two began seeing one another regularly at first only to discuss the tenets of Nichiren Shoshu Sokagakkai . . . but eventually to discuss their feelings about one another. 'She was still married, so we were very quietly having this affair,' Patrick told author Jackie Collins on a segment of the American TV show *Entertainment Tonight*. Once, he said, 'we went to a friend's wedding up in Maine. We snuck out of this little cabin we were in and took a blanket. It was raining, and we went on a walk in the woods, and we laid down on the blanket and made love.' It became quickly apparent to Patrick that the oohing and aahing noises Carlyn was making were the result more of pain than pleasure. 'Under the blanket were these pine cones,' he laughed.

'We still have those pine cones today.'

Patrick became fascinated by the practice of Buddhism as Carlyn espoused it. She explained to him that repeating a prescribed mantra while visualizing a goal made it possible to attain that goal. To a 22-year-old, it seemed as simple as wishing on a star, or trading molars for dollars with the Tooth Fairy. Surely it couldn't actually help – but then again, it couldn't *hurt*. He began joining the dancer as she chanted.

He chanted for Carlyn's love, and he chanted for the return of his voice. Although he was able to audibly croak by now, he had been told in no uncertain terms that a fully rounded speaking voice would probably never return to him; his career as an actor seemed to be over before it had begun.

Within ten weeks, Patrick's voice returned. (He even

invited his doom-saying doctor to his comeback stage performance.) Chanting worked! In 1972, Patrick moved in with Carlyn. Chanting *really* worked. Patrick wrote a note to his parents:

'I am going to New York to live with a married ballerina who is 10 years older than I am.

'P.S. I am a Buddhist.'

As one can imagine, the response of the senior Duffys was less than enthusiastic. An acquaintance of Terrence recalls, 'Duff was a hunting-shooting-fishing kind of guy, a pick-up-truck-and-trailer man, and he expected his son to grow up in similar fashion. And here he embraces this kooky religion – not even a religion in the purest sense, but a flakey Hollywood kind of Buddhism where you chant for fame and fortune and fancy cars.

'Patrick tried to explain to his dad that it was okay to chant for the things you wanted out of life, that it was okay to ask the Buddha for success and material possessions, that by chanting this nimmy-nammy-ho-ho stuff you put yourself in attunement with the universe and good things happen.

'It was all incomprehensible to Duff. This was a guy who believed in meat-and-potatoes Christianity: going to Church and getting down on your knees. The closest he would come to chanting is saying the catechism. His son seemed strange and distant to him all of a sudden. Duff would go over to his friend's bar across the street sometimes, and just scratch his head in wonderment and amazement.'

Terrence and Marie would continue to snub Carlyn Duffy and her religious beliefs for the next 15 years.

'How can an Irishman be a Buddhist?' moaned Terrence to a friend.

One should pause here a moment to understand exactly what Nichiren Shoshu Sokagakkai of America – abbreviated as NSA – really does encompass, since it has been the single biggest influence and motivating force in Patrick Duffy's life for these past 15 years. Most Westerners dismiss it just as Terrence Duffy did: mystic mumbo-jumbo for acquisitive airheads. Even observers with an appreciation of Oriental philosophies have said 'Nishiren Shoshu is to Buddhism what Terry Cole Whittaker is to Christianity. They should all wear buttons that say "God *wants* me to have a VCR."'

Patrick Duffy just isn't that shallow . . . as his father, eventually, would come to understand.

This sect of Buddhism was founded in Japan in the year 1200 by Nichiren Daishonin, and is called in English the 'Practice of the Rising Sun.' While the scope of Buddhist philosophy can hardly be encapsulated in a single sentence, the core of NSA teaching is this: It is possible to attune oneself to the harmony of the universe and attain a higher life condition by chanting the words *nam-myoho-renge-kyo*. Literally translated, the mantra consists of: *nam* – 'dedication'; *myoho* – 'the mystic laws' or essential principles of the universe; *renge* – 'the lotus flower,' which symbolizes the inevitability of cause and effect; and *kyo* – 'the Sutra,' or teachings of the Buddha.

Strung together and loosely translated, the mantra declares: 'I devote myself to the inexpressably profound and wonderful truth, expounded in the Lotus Sutra, which embodies the loftiest teachings of Buddhism.'

'To the Western mind I know this all sounds very mystical,' says Diane Newberry, a fellow NSA member who began practising the same year Patrick did. 'But this is a very down-to-earth, common-sense and logical philosophy. *Renge*, cause and effect, is synonymous with karma, a term we're all familiar with. According to Buddhism, chanting *nam-myoho-renge-kyo*, the ultimate law, develops a natural rhythm and enables a person to tap their highest life condition – which is enlightenment.

'It's a concrete tool that people can use in their daily lives,' she continues. 'You use it to raise your life condition to a point where you see things differently. You see opportunities where there were none, you actually change things for the better. Not through changing your environment – through changing yourself.'

The officials at NSA headquarters in Santa Monica, California, say that there are 22 million Nichiren Buddhists around the world, including 500,000 families in the U.S. who practise regularly. (Other studies have put U.S. membership estimates as low as 30,000). The Beverly Hills chapter alone, in which Patrick became a leading figure, boasts almost 2,000 members – many of them very familiar names. Outspoken NSA devotees in Los Angeles include music stars Tina Turner, Herbie Hancock, Quincy Jones and Stevie Wonder. Diane Newberry herself is a successful singer in her own right (and with enough chanting, who knows?).

'Members come from all walks of life,' says Newberry. 'In one meeting you'll find Japanese, Chinese,

Indian, black, white – from all different economic backgrounds.' Some members think of Nichiren Buddhism as their religion; others consider it a philosophy and continue to call themselves Protestants – or Lutherans or Baptists or whatever – even while they chant. NSA does not require its followers to become vegetarians, conscientious objectors, celibates, teetotallers, fitness enthusiasts or financial supporters of the temple. It only requires a commitment to chant every morning and every evening.

The Duffys, along with every other NSA follower, start each morning with *daimoku* (chanting the mantra) in front of a *butsudan* containing the *gohonzon*. That's an intimidating way of saying they meditate while looking at a piece of paper. The *gohonzon* is a replica of the scroll inscribed by Nichiren Daishonin in the village of Kominato almost 800 years ago. A *butsudan* is the altar that holds it. Included in the ritual are candles (for the sense of sight), a gong (hearing), and incense (smell) and beads (touch). Evergreens are placed alongside the *butsudan* to represent the eternity of life. There is no required posture for chanting, no set length of time one must chant and, above all, no stipulations about what you may or may not chant for.

'Happiness is different things to different people,' says Newberry. 'People start out chanting for a car or a better job but as time goes on and they continue the practice, their value system begins to change. I've seen it happen often. It doesn't matter what you start chanting for, because the law is true. Over time, that person's life condition will raise. Their rhythm will get stronger. In Buddhism, happiness is a combination of physical, mental and spiritual well-being. And no matter how completely materialistic a person is, no one can embrace this philosophy and not be changed by it.'

'Buddhism has had nothing but a positive effect on almost every aspect of my existence,' says Patrick. 'I relate to everything – the way I approach everything, my attitude towards it – through my practice of Buddhism. My system of values, the priorities of my life, are based on the way I feel because I am a practising Buddhist.'

At first, Patrick was one of the very people his temple-mates referred to as 'completely materialistic.' And her prediction that no one can stick with the practice and remain unchanged has certainly proved out in his case. After all, the man started out chanting for a roll in the hay with a pretty ballerina!

'In the East, this is perfectly understandable,' explained Duffy. 'If people don't have food, they chant for food. If they don't have an automobile, they chant for an automobile. If they can't find the right woman, they chant for the right woman. There is nothing wrong with that.'

But, as he found along the line, 'If somebody needs to be told "If you want a new car, chant for it," why shouldn't they chant for it – if it will instigate the Buddha nature to start showing itself in all other areas of their lives. Eventually, they are going to realize that the car is not the source of their unhappiness. The source of their unhappiness lies somewhere else – but in chanting for the car, they gained the wisdom to see that.'

Now, he says, 'If I need energy, I chant for energy. If I need to calm down, I chant to calm down. If there's something in your environment negative to you, you don't have to change your environment. You change yourself.

'You assume total responsibility for your life.'

4

Diving In The Deep End

'I've never stepped on a stage,' says Patrick Duffy, 'where just before going on I didn't think, "This is it; this is where I commit suicide. I'm going to walk out there and they're going to look at me and I'm going to be on the next bus . . . I'm getting out of here!"'

But those fears were easily overwhelmed by Patrick's compulsion to succeed as a performer. What are a few butterflies compared to the ecstasy of approbation, the giddy sensation of applause? Many of us grow up convinced that we are somehow different, something special – destined for more than the mundane fates meted out to those around us. As children, it seems, we're all convinced that we were somehow stolen from royal nurseries, exchanged by fairies with a common babe – or, in an interchangeable scenario, know that some day our prince will come. Few of us ever prove the changelings we dream ourselves to be.

The dirt-poor barman's son from Montana was determined to grab his star . . . to be a star. He would, and did, exhaust all logical steps – and a few metaphysical ones – to achieve his goal. He was perfectly willing to work twice as hard as anyone had a right to expect. But, as Patrick recalled in 1977, it was finally Carlyn who forced him to chase down his grail. 'She said, "You want to be an actor? Well, get off your ass and get out of Seattle!"'

Patrick and Carlyn moved to New York City and set up housekeeping as what the U.S. Census Bureau romantically calls POSSLQ's: Persons of Opposite Sex Sharing Living Quarters. Carlyn, waiting out a final divorce decree, more or less supported both of them on her salary from the First Chamber Dance Company. Patrick picked up pin money teaching exercise classes for her colleagues, and worked as a part-time bartender and waiter. 'The other waiters used to scrape leftover food off the plates for me to take home,' is Patrick's pithy description of the couple's financial circumstances.

'They lived in a tiny apartment,' remembers one of the Duffys' friends. 'There were so many cockroaches that they had to keep the lights turned on at night – because if the lights were off, the place would be overrun.'

It was a frustrating time, and the frustrations took their toll on the deepening relationship between Patrick and Carlyn. To put it bluntly – as Patrick Duffy himself did, twice, on national television – he cheated on her.

'I was 22, and not a mature 22,' he said on *The Tonight Show*. 'I wasn't mentally set, I think, for one person.' Johnny Carson, and his millions of viewers, listened intently as Patrick bared his soul and his youthful views on love, marriage and fidelity (even though he was fudging a bit on his age!). His relationship with Carlyn, felt his younger self, 'just seemed like dating, only more serious. And I blew it.'

As he told Barbara Walters (during prime time, no less), 'We were going through a bad set of circumstances, and it shook our whole relationship right to the core. And made us both stand up and say, "This is much too valuable to play with."

'We went through some pretty tough times, and we survived them.'

Through a rededication to Buddha and to each other, Patrick and Carlyn cemented their relationship. Today, Patrick Duffy readily admits to retaining his interest in attractive women: He will flirt, he will wink, he will admire and he will smile . . but he will not stray. And this is not a matter of religious conviction; as Patrick told Tom Green of *USA Today*, 'There are no rules. I don't do drugs because I don't do drugs – but I didn't do drugs before I became a Buddhist. I eat red meat. There's nothing within this sect of Buddhism that regulates your life in any way. If I were so inclined, I could have an affair. But I'm not so inclined.'

A mystically oriented person – a person like, say, Carlyn Rosser Duffy – might consider it 'karma' that a light at the end of the tunnel should appear in Patrick's career right about this time. Whether or not it was a reward for his spiritual growth and newfound moral rectitude, the light did make itself known. Patrick was cast in an off-Broadway production of William Inge's *Natural Affection*.

It wasn't a big part, and it wasn't a big production,

but it was a good play. And Patrick wrote to every theatrical agent he knew – or knew someone who knew someone who knew – inviting them to come see his work.

Perseverence paid off ('Stick it out, as long as it takes' is Duffy's standard advice to aspiring actors). An agent named Joan Scott came to see the performance. She and her partner, Grace Smith, signed Patrick on the spot – and have represented him ever since. The Writers and Artists Agency is today collecting a tidy percentage of a multi-million-dollar income; the agency itself has become but one division of 'Joan Scott, Inc.' It was the kind of signing that industry types call either 'blind luck' or 'infallible instinct' . . . depending on their degree of friendship with the signatories.

All Joan and Grace had in 1973, though, was an unknown with great looks and tons of potential. And for Patrick, even the coup of landing a real live agent was no guarantee of screen stardom. After *Natural Affection*, Patrick didn't get another acting part for almost three years. Ironically, those very good looks were working against him. When you're topping 6′ 3″ in boots – not to mention all that bushy dark hair – and the star of the production you audition for is 5′ 8″, you're suddenly an unpopular choice for the job. 'Being tall . . . it has hurt,' admitted Patrick on an episode of *Donahue*. 'I'm sure it was a factor in my unemployment.'

While waiting for a break, he continued teaching class for Carlyn's ballet company, as well as 'cooking her meals and drawing her baths.' Ironically, the ballet company at this point opened a West Coast workshop back in Seattle, of all places. Patrick and Carlyn got on a plane and headed back to square one.

Coincidence piled on coincidence (or was it the chanting that did it?), as Joan Scott now decided to open an agency branch office in L.A. 'She called me in Seattle,' said Patrick, 'and suggested I try Hollywood.'

Patrick and Carlyn celebrated by getting married in a Buddhist temple; she wore flowers in her hair and a blue-and-white checked cotton dress, while he was 'formally' attired in an unbuttoned safari shirt over a turtleneck. But hey, it was 1974. The sun had barely set on Woodstock; the arrival of son Padraic (Irish for 'Patrick') was 10½ months away; and the newlyweds were happily living on love, hope and spinach casseroles. Finally, they were in Hollywood!

HOLLYWOOD. It has a magical sound, an aura that gives a backlit shimmer to the very letters in its name. But below the letters of that famous sign atop Beachwood Canyon Drive is a section of urban blight no film producer ever really wants to capture on celluloid. Hollywood, the town, is nothing like Hollywood, the image. And the Duffys lived right in the middle of Hollywood, the town.

'They lived in a seedy, one-room apartment,' recalled Bonita Ann Miller, who would become the Duffy's housekeeper-in-residence in later, fatter years. 'To get to the front door, they had to step over the winos and drunks.' Patrick got a job driving a truck, delivering floral arrangements to the homes of *successful* actors. Joan Scott and her friends kept him in odd jobs, 'mowing their lawns, rebuilding their kitchens, putting new roofs on their houses – anything to keep the rent paid.' He was, as he told the New York *Post* in 1982, 'biding my time and keeping body and soul together until what I assumed would happen did happen.'

But without a Screen Actors Guild card, you can't get an acting job. And without an acting job, you can't get a SAG card. Patrick was caught in show business's most infamous Catch-22.

Thanks to Joan Scott's casting-director friends, Patrick did finally get enough work to join the union – although not nearly enough work to supported Carlyn and baby Padraic. He earned a walk-on role in a television movie-of-the-week starring Beau Bridges called *The Stranger Who Looks Like Me*, and another bit part in the teleflick *Hurricane*. And then his classical training paid off in 1975 when he was taken on for the summer season of the San Diego Old Globe Shakespeare Company. It was 100 miles away from his doorstep, but it was a respectable gig in the milieu he knew best. And it beat the hell out of $3 an hour for delivering flowers.

'He did *The Tempest* and *Measure for Measure* and *Much Ado About Nothing*,' says Bill Eaton, who was – and still is – publicity director for the Old Globe. 'The shows were in a rotating repertory system.

'I remember clearly when we first met,' says Eaton, 'because it was such a strange coincidence. He was with a very attractive young lady. I must have been looking at her oddly, because he said to me, "You remember my wife, Carlyn?" And then I realized that

she was the girl who had played the lead in our production of the musical *On The Town* back in 1958. She
hadn't been back since. She must have been a teenager
the last time I saw her, and here she was with a baby in
her arms!'

Duffy and the Old Globe got on well together. 'We
thought of Patrick as being conscientious, hard-
working, committed and very anxious to learn,' says
Eaton. Today, the San Diegans point to their colleague
with the same glow as do the residents of Boulder,
Montana: 'We're very proud of him.'

Returning to Los Angeles in the autumn of '75,
Patrick got quite a nice role as Julie Harris's nephew in
a PBS production of *The Last of Mrs. Lincoln*. He
auditioned for *Star Wars*, but was rejected. (Duffy
mistook director George Lucas for a fellow wanna-be
in the waiting room, and 'probably said something
rude to him.') He got a small part in the Robert
Wagner/Eddie Albert TV series *Switch*, and was one
of 500 auditioned for the lead in a new NBC science
fiction show called *Man From Atlantis*. He was
turned down: too skinny, they said, and they really
wanted a 'name' athlete for the part.

Two months after he lost the role of Mark Harris,
sole survivor of an ancient underwater civilization,
Duffy got another call from casting director Ruth Conforte. She had just seen his episode of *Switch*, and
realized he was more suited for the part than she had
imagined. Duffy, then working for carpenter's wages
constructing a houseboat, was called in for another
screen test.

'I didn't have enough money to buy a swimming

suit,' Patrick has recalled with giggles on many occasions, 'so I had to do the audition in my underwear.' As well as his BVD's , he wore a padded sweater, to cheat up his 11st 11lb physique. They screen-tested him dry and they screen-tested him wet, and he puffed up his too-skinny chest until he thought it would explode – especially during the longer underwater scenes. But he had a certain sinuous strength that struck producer Herb Solow (formerly of *Star Trek* and *Mission: Impossible*) as somehow *Atlantean*, and he had good chemistry with co-star Belinda Montgomery. He was personable, persevering, and pleased as punch to work for $3,000 per show. Two days before shooting began, he got the part.

Man From Atlantis was initially signed for four two-hour episodes as a summer replacement at the end of the 1976–77 season. When episode number four logged in at No. 1 on the week's Neilsen rating, it was immediately picked up for a 13-week contract beginning the following autumn. For the first time, Patrick and Carlyn would have enough money to raise their son in a comfortable (or, to credit casting director Ruth – whose name will appear in these pages again – should that be 'Conforte-able'?) environment. But the work had just begun.

The main order of business was for Patrick to transform himself into Mark Harris . . . if not Mark Spitz. Number one on the agenda was to gain ten pounds (preferably twenty pounds) by Monday (preferably *last* Monday.) Veteran stuntman Paul Stader, who had doubled for every swimmer from Johnny 'Tarzan'

Weismuller to Lloyd 'Sea Hunt' Bridges, put Patrick on a regime of high-protein drinks and daily weight training, as well as instructing him in the ways of a world-class swimmer. Patrick, it turns out, hadn't so much as jumped into a pool for five years before landing the *Atlantis* job. A day in the life started at 4:30 a.m. with chanting, then an hour of isometrics and pumping iron, followed by a full-body shave – Patrick's least favourite part.

First call at the saucer-shaped water tank outside MGM Studios in Culver City was 6:30 a.m., which meant sitting still for 90 minutes while 'Mr Spock's' *Star Trek* make-up man, Fred Phillips, glued webs to Duffy's hands and covered his body in Max Factor 'light Egyptian' pancake. (That's the shade Lena Horne used to joke about, saying Hollywood had developed it for her to wear in *Showboat* . . . 'and then they went out and slapped it all over Ava Gardner instead!')

Mark Harris's finger-webs alone took an hour to apply: Five coats of latex were painted onto a mould of Patrick's hands, allowed to dry and then slowly worked over his own fingers. The procedure was so trying that Patrick would eat lunch wearing his webs sooner than have them reapplied – a habit that caused commissary silverware to drop frequently from both his own fingers and those of startled onlookers.

The final indignity in becoming Mark Harris was the pair of fluorescent lime-green contact lenses that covered not only the naturally hazel iris, but the entire visible portion of Patrick's eyeballs. Irritating to the point of being agonizing, each lens was the size of a 5p coin; co-star Victor Buono observed sympathetically that for poor Patrick it was like 'acting with golf balls stuck in your head.'

'It nearly killed me,' is how Patrick summed up his work on *Man From Atlantis*. Not that he didn't like the part; he did. Duffy identified with the otherworldly, kindly Harris: 'I find him extremely, intelligently naïve,' said Patrick. 'He's unencumbered by hang-ups and idiosyncracies. He has a total lack of that kind of ego that stops us from taking a different direction because we hate to admit that the one we took in the first place was wrong.'

Many times, an actor comes to hate a television series job because the work isn't demanding enough of his acting skills. This would, in fact, become a factor in Patrick's career a few years later. Now, however, the problem was one of a part being *too* demanding – not on Patrick's talent, but on his body.

Even though Duffy was a decent – if rusty – swimmer, the swimming required in *Atlantis* was a different kettle of, ah, fish than the swimming you do in your pool. Mark Harris wouldn't be a believable alien doing the Australian crawl or the backstroke. No, in order to give the impression that Harris was a naturally seagoing creature, Patrick had to swim more like a porpoise than a person. Duffy was trained in an up-and-down undulation that started at the top of his head and progressed in a wave to the tip of his toes. And since the human backbone stops at the hip (unlike the backbone of a dolphin), which goes all the way to the tailfin), this procedure became increasingly excruciating for the actor.

'It's tiring, especially in the base of your back,'

Patrick told *TV Guide* with enormous under-statement. 'And it's not too good for you to swim that way.'

Then there was the small matter of talking while totally immersed. In character as a waterbreather (Mark Harris turned purple if exposed to the air for more than a few hours), Patrick would first hyperven-tilate oxygen and then plunge beneath the surface, opening his mouth to 'speak' while never letting so much as a bubble of the carefully hoarded air escape his lips. 'You inhale just enough water to go up into your nose and sinuses so that no air comes out.' Ugh! This was all done to a script, of course, and the words later dubbed in with appropriate watery distortion.

When you're on location 60 feet below sea level off the coast of Catalina Island, breathing ocean water that's down to 57 degrees Farenheit, there's more pressure on you – literally and figuratively – than worrying about hitting your mark or blowing a line. You're worrying about dying.

'You get this feeling underwater, you hallucinate and you think you can breathe,' Duffy told *Starlog* magazine. 'You get panicked and all you can hear is your heart thumping. Once, I thought: "I'm not going to make it!" All of a sudden, a very tranquil feeling came over me and I thought, "I can stay here forever."'

After about 30 minutes of underwater work, the cameramen/divers (who, unlike bare-chested Patrick, worked in the warmth of wet-suits) would pull the actor back up to the real world, rub down his twitching muscles and force-feed him hot soup.

But Duffy enjoyed his months under the sea, for the

most part. 'I was working all the time and I like that, because I'm a workaholic,' he said. 'It was virtually a one-man show.' He even got to such a point of under-water proficiency that he personally completed 80% of the required stunt-work – simply because no one else around could do the stunts as well. (He also lived in fear that some impressionable fan would tie an andiron around his neck and throw him off a bridge, but that's another nightmare!)

And, of course, $3,000 a week is a fortune to someone who's been living off his wife's income as, at that time, a ballet instructor at a Santa Monica school. Carlyn was able to give up teaching to stay home with Padraic and manage the Duffy finances. The family even was able to take a vacation trip to Hawaii, giving Patrick a chance to relive some of his Mark Harris stunts . . . with the luxury of a snorkle.

He discovered, for the first time, what it meant to have public recognition for his talent – and what the obverse of that delightful phenomenon can become. NBC once asked him to do a promotional tape for the series, and he happily brought the camera crews into his home and put toddler Padraic in the picture. Days later, Carlyn went into a local store and the proprietor looked at her son and said 'Gee, isn't that the same boy I saw on TV with Patrick Duffy?'

Patrick Duffy never exposed his family to that glaring light again. He was no less interested in it for himself, however; finally, he was becoming a 'face.' Once an actor has regular prime-time visibility, it means getting his name and picture in newspapers and magazines – and the self-perpetuating cycle of celebrity begins its ever-increasing spiral. Extra income would come from jobs like hosting the National Auto Show in New York City, jobs never offered to players with the Old Globe Theatre.

'I remember photographing him when he was appearing at that Auto Show in New York,' says celebrity photographer Russell Turiak. 'He was friendly, smiling, signing autographs – no big star trip at all.

'Of course, he wasn't much of anybody back then, anyway. But I've always found him to be the same: pleasant, unpretentious, never full of himself.

'The only thing he doesn't like is to be called "Pat." I remember pointing the camera at him and saying "Hey, Pat!" And his look could have killed. He said, slowly and clearly, 'My name is *Patrick.*"'

Well, *Patrick* was finally getting the outside verification of his belief in himself – and Carlyn's belief in him – that he needed. As he said in a 1982 interview, the most difficult moment in deciding to attempt an acting career is when you have to 'look at yourself realistically and be honest. Are you really good enough to make a career out of it? If you can't be honest, the industry has its own weeding-out process.'

Duffy had survived the first cut. And even though *Man From Atlantis* only survived the 13 weeks of its 1977 contract, it went on to become one of the first American television programmes to air in mainland China, debuting in Peking on 3 February, 1980. In 1987, Mark Harris is more popular in Japan than even Bobby Ewing. '"Bllubb-bllubb" is the same in any language,' laughs Patrick.

Unfortunately, the *Man From Atlantis* contract

didn't award its titular player a penny for foreign residuals, a negotiating oversight that became a bitter pill for Duffy ... but a valuable learning experience about the business of show business. 'I was brainwashed into thinking I was lucky to be working at all,' Duffy later sighed. 'I was paid as little as any actor in a starring role could possibly be.'

One week after *Man From Atlantis* was cancelled, Patrick was offered five different scripts for upcoming TV projects. 'At that point it was a crap-shoot,' he recalled. "Carlyn and I said, "Let's chant for a while." So we chanted and said, "That one."'

There were 12 other tall, dark and handsome men auditioning for 'that one.' We all know who got the part. And we all know what 'that one' was.

5

The Birth of Dallas

In 1977, screenwriter David Jacobs considered himself
a lucky man. With only a year and a half of experience in
the television industry, he was holding down a good job
as story editor for the critically acclaimed series *Family*.
An unusually heartfelt drama, the 1976–80 ABC series
launched the careers of Meredith Baxter-Birney, Kristy
McNichol and Gary Frank, and set a standard for
homely realism and affectionate relationships still felt
in current hits from *Hill Street Blues* to *The Cosby
Show*.

But, like Patrick Duffy, David Jacobs had big dreams
– and his biggest dream was to create a television series
he could call his own.

Jacobs teamed up with Mike Filerman, a staffer at the
Lorimar Productions think tank (called 'project development executive' in industry jargon), and started
working up a fresh prime-time concept, a departure
from the cops and doctors mould of the day. Jacobs
wanted to make an Americanized version of Ingmar
Bergman's 'Scenes From A Marriage.' Filerman was

more inclined toward co-opting the sexploitation flicks popular on the drive-in circuit. Their compromise became the treatment for *Knots Landing*, a sudsy melodrama set in California.

CBS network brass liked this idea for a series centered around four modern families and their convoluted interrelationships. But they worried that the setting was 'too middle-class.' Could Jacobs rewrite the treatment with another coat of gloss, an extra dollop of pizzazz? Throw in more money, more glamour, more decadence. Oh, and write in a part for Linda Evans, please, because we've got her under contract.

Maybe we could move Knots Landing to the Southwest? Now *there's* a region that's absolutely booming, the Next Big Thing. How about setting the show in sprawling, brawling Texas, awash with oil and brash with riches? Houston, maybe? San Antonio? Forth Worth?

How about . . . Dallas?

David Jacobs has often insisted that half the credit for dreaming up *Dallas* belongs to the CBS exec – 'director of drama programme development,' technically speaking – who made all these suggestions.

'*Dallas* was really Richard Burger's idea,' said the cherubic Jacobs in *The Complete Book of Dallas*. Under the working title 'Untitled Linda Evans Project' (she was to have played Pam!), the relocated *Knots Landing* began to take shape. Jacobs liked the new setting, particularly as he was currently reading the Tommy Thompson bestseller *Blood and Money*, which also took place in the area.

Jacobs told Filerman that he was raring to go, ready

to catch the next plane to Dallas and research his relocated location. Recalled Jacobs, 'He [Filerman] talked me out of it. "CBS is hot for this script," he said "Let's get it in as quickly as possible. Go to Dallas *after*."'

And so David Jacobs wrote a 'bible' for a television series set in a town he had never visited, fleshing out the lives and backgrounds of people he envisioned by stereotype, Thompsonia and his fond memories of an old friend from Waco named . . . Pamela.

The first draft of 'Untitled Linda Evans Project' was dated 10 December 1977. At the last moment, Filerman crossed that out and substituted the name 'Dallas.' 'We can always change it again,' he laughed.

Six weeks later, David Jacobs was finally in Texas, filming the series pilot plus four additional episodes. He discovered that he was wrong about one minor point in his original script: far from being a city constantly roasting under the Texas sun, as Jacobs described it, the real Dallas in January of 1978 was covered by four feet of snow.

Jacobs and producer Leonard Katzman – along with Mike Filerman's Lorimar successor, Phil Capice – found one additional pivotal matter where fiction and fact refused to coincide. There was, it turned out, not a single viable oil well in Dallas County. The solution was simple: they invented Braddock County, home of Southfork Ranch and root of the Ewing family fortune.

It would not be the last time that the history of *Dallas* had to bend to the Procrustean bed of reality . . . or vice versa.

The five-part pilot, while neither a serial nor a mini-series, was an attempt to give viewers enough time with the main characters – 'the family Ewing and those people who are married to, sleeping with or fighting with them,' as Leonard Katzman describes it – to clutch them to their collective bosom. One hour wouldn't begin to scratch the surface, felt CBS. Jacobs personally wrote Episodes One and Five, and writers Virginia Aldridge, Arthur Bernard Lewis and Camille Marchetta were hired for Two through Four.

Bobby Ewing was scheduled to die at the end of Episode Five.

The Ewing saga – the 'historical' background of the family – was conceived as follows:

It was in the 1850s that Enoch Southworth bought up 100,000 acres of barely arable land 35 miles north of the fledgling city called Dallas. It was too dry and salty to farm, but it was suitable for grazing cattle. By 1870, Southfork Ranch (named for the branching river it straddled) has become one of the most prosperous in the territory. A proud Enoch has fathered a son named Aaron, and instituted a tradition that stands unto this day: The annual Southfork Barbeque.

After the turn of the century, longhorns give way to Herefords. Horses give way to automobiles. And cattle slowly give way to the 'black gold' that seeps from the Texas soil. Enoch extracts a promise from Aaron: Never will an oil well be drilled on Southfork land. And then he dies.

Aaron marries, and fathers two children: Garrison and Eleanor. It is his daughter, Ellie, rather than his son, who followed in Aaron's footsteps. It is she who

holds back tears while she nurses calves struck down
by anthrax; it is she who trembles when the drought of
1930 threatens their very livelihood. And it is she who
stands by her father in his refusal to drill for oil on
Southfork.

In 1933, the tomboyish hellion Ellie Southworth is
keeping Southfork alive by sheer force of will. Her
neighbour and childhood sweetheart, Willard Barnes,
has left the section of Southfork land that Aaron had
deeded to the boy's late father, and is seeking his
fortune in the burgeoning oil fields. Willard isn't good
for much – self-destructive, alcoholic, both impulsive
and compulsive – but he has an uncanny, even mystical, knack for smelling out oil.

When he meets a wildcatter named John Ross 'Jock'
Ewing (the meeting taking place when Jock saves
Willard's skin), the pair team up in an attempt to strike
it rich. With 'Digger' Barnes's nose and Jock Ewing's
strength and business savvy complementing one
another, the pair beat the odds and become overnight
millionaires.

Jock Ewing is a giant of a man. We don't know much
about where he comes from: We know he has an
unreliable big brother, Jason, and an incurably insane
wife, Amanda. We also know that he is honourable,
moral, ethical, honest, loyal, polite, brave, totally lack-
ing in prejudice and instantly smitten by Ellie
Southworth. Ellie, desperate to save her home from
the auction block, is determined to marry her now-
solvent former boyfriend. She reacts to Jock Ewing like
a cat reacts to a bathtub.

Thanks to his 'damn honour,' as brother Jason calls

it, Jock promises to do everything possible to help poor Digger win the heart of Miss Ellie. 'I'm gonna give you all the help I can,' he says to his drunken partner as he pours away every drop of booze. 'But if you do find a way, Digger Barnes – if you do mess up . . . she's mine.'

Digger, naturally, does the very thing that can hurt him most, throwing Jock's friendship in his face and running away. And those sparks flying between Jock and Ellie prove to be fire of another kind. Ellie is pregnant with John Ross Ewing, Jr. when Jock secretly goes to Amanda and asks for his freedom. The marriage of Jock and Ellie produces J.R., and two years later another son, Garrison ('Gary'). In 1948, along comes Bobby.

Digger, still his own worst enemy, gets married and soon abandons two children, Cliff and Pam. His sister Maggie tries to raise them, and the young ones all watch the fateful scene when Digger becomes a most unwelcome guest at the annual barbeque in 1951. On that day Digger Barnes tries to murder Jock Ewing. On that day Digger realizes that there is a fortune in oil under his birthright section of Southfork land – the same section he had drunkenly challenged Aaron Southworth to buy from him a decade before for a quick $1000.

Digger Barnes, happily, doesn't succeed in shooting Jock Ewing. But he does succeed in establishing a Hatfield-McCoy feud between the two clans that is to escalate year after year. Someday, the mantle will pass to Cliff and Pam and J.R. and Bobby.

April 1978: It's been almost 40 years since a Barnes has spoken civilly to a Ewing. So when Bobby James

Ewing marries Pamela Jean Barnes after a whirlwind courtship in New Orleans, it is the worst thing he could do to his family honour. And hours after he drives his new bride to Southfork in his sporty Mercedes 450 SL, brother J.R. is already trying to buy Pammy off. Or compromise her with ranch foreman Ray Krebbs, who had been her sweetheart in the past. None of this is going to work: Pamela Barnes Ewing is strong-willed, strong-minded and strongly bonded to the man she has married.

Treated as an outcast in her in-laws' home, Pam nonetheless becomes peacemaker and problem-solver. She keeps rebellious teen niece Lucy Ewing (who is coincidentally fooling around with Ray Krebbs) from lying herself into even more trouble. Pam acts as liaison between her bitter brother and the Ewings, preventing Cliff – now counsel for a state senate investigating committee – from destroying Ewing Oil. She stands with the terrified Ewing women when a disgruntled cuckold seeks revenge on his wife's presumed lover, J.R., by attacking the Southfork wives.

And she happily announces to her beloved Bobby that she is pregnant with the first Ewing grandchild. In eight years, J.R. and his former-Miss Texas wife, Sue Ellen, have been unable to conceive. It's *inconceivable*, thinks Sue Ellen, that this outsider should present Jock with an heir. J.R. at first tries to convince Bobby that the child is Ray Krebbs's. Unsuccesful, he picks a fight with Pam at the annual barbeque. And when she falls from a hayloft, she loses her precious baby.

But in a way, Pam has won. Comforting her in her sadness, begging her and Bobby not to leave Southfork, Miss Ellie says to her: 'I need your help, Pamela. Please.'

'In the beginning, we called it "Pammy Solves All",' laughed Leonard Katzman. The first five episodes of *Dallas* – each of which were complete unto themselves, neither a serial nor a mini-series – were predicated on the conflicts arising when a girl from the wrong side of the tracks marries into a rich Texas family.

'Pamela was the protagonist, and J.R. was the antagonist' – this was the basic dramatic set-up as described by David Jacobs. Bobby was meant to be something of a prodigal son, rather than a knight in shining armor, and Cliff Barnes was made in the noble political mould of John F. Kennedy. Sue Ellen Shepard Ewing was little more than a cipher: 'The brunette on the couch,' Katzman used to call her. The only really decent person on the show was Miss Ellie.

But the CBS brass were taken with Bobby Ewing's character. They saw him as Good opposed to J.R.'s Evil. Cain vs. Abel, they felt, was a stronger conflict than Montague vs. Capulet. So the season-closer that was to have removed Bobby Ewing from the show permanently, ended up removing his unborn child instead. And 'Pammy Saves All' metamorphosed into 'Leave It To Bobby.'

Dallas began airing on Sunday evenings at 10 p.m., for five weeks in a row starting 2 April 1978. The show's early audience acceptance was lukewarm, to say the least; it entered the Neilsen charts at a bottom-brushing No. 58. The five-show pilot run logged in at a cumulative 17th place, but that wasn't bad enough to scare off network programmers. Production company Lorimar was then mining gold with their two other hits, 'Eight Is Enough' and 'The Waltons,' and CBS had faith in the firm's track record. Still, as Patrick Duffy remembered it, 'Every actor in the show was looking for other work after we shot the five episodes.'

On Show Number Five, the inituitive gamble that audiences would develop a to-know-them-is-to-love-them attitude about the denizens of Southfork paid off. The final pilot hour cracked the Neilsen weekly Top Ten, and *Dallas* was renewed for thirteen episodes to lead off the new autumn season. Year One of the *Dallas* phenomenon was about to begin.

The cast that has made *Dallas* so real over the past decade was hardly set in stone back then. Even Patrick Duffy didn't have a lock on the part of Bobby Ewing: it was once considered for actor Steve Kanaly ('Ray Krebbs'), and Ken Kercheval ('Cliff Barnes') would have been Ray. After Linda Evans was deemed too heavyweight, box-office-wise, for the part of Pam, the contract became a close contest between Victoria Principal and daytime soapstar Judith Chapman. Principal got the part, and Evans got her place in the soaper hierarchy with the upcoming 'Dynasty.'

The role of Sue Ellen almost went to Mary Frann, later a co-star of *The Bob Newhart Show*. Larry Hagman, who had made a pilot for a series called *Three's Company* (no relation to the ABC sitcom with that title) the same season, was almost replaced by Robert

Foxworth – who would himself eventually star in another prime-time serial, *Falcon Crest*.

Some cast changes occurred mid-stream. Digger Barnes, originally played by David Wayne, was later played by Keenan Wynn. Morgan Fairchild was an early 'Jenna Wade,' later replaced by Priscilla Beaulieu Presley. Middle brother Gary Ewing was portrayed by actor David Ackroyd before the reins were handed to Ted Shackelford – who took them and rode right out to California, starting a spin-off series called (of course) *Knots Landing*.

Like the very title *Dallas*, everything about the early shows was subject to change. 'We were staying at a little motel in Texas called the North Park Inn,' recalls Duffy. 'And after every day's shooting, Leonard Katzman's phone would ring and I'd say "Let's have coffee." And we'd meet in the coffee shop, and the next day he'd be typing new pages.' Patrick had Katzman's ear, and he had some very definite ideas about the direction his still-malleable character should take. 'I could have been the second bad son or the tormented son. But I didn't think that worked,' says Patrick. 'At the start, Bobby was ineffectual – blind to the realities of his own family and his own situation. I said, "Come on, guys. We've got to make him smarter, tougher, more of a realist – or the audience won't side with him."

'It's tough to write for the good guy. Bobby got the short end of the stick.'

Because as hard as Patrick worked on Bobby Ewing, and as much as Bobby was the dramatic favourite of everyone involved in the show (except creator Jacobs, who has said he still wishes the character had been killed off in the first year), the fact is that *Dallas* didn't become a mega-hit based on the Man You Love to Love.

Dallas became a mega-hit because of the Man You Love to Hate.

6

Over The Top

'Our show is based on reality,' says producer Leonard Katzman. 'Los Angeles has a palm tree on every corner, so we film in Texas. We use probably 100 to 150 local actors, two thousand to three thousand extras, and sixty percent of the location crew is local. We have a commitment to a look, a feel of the show.'

The commitment required, in many respects, is greater for the creation of *Dallas* than it is for most prime-time series. Television jobs, on the average, are rather like teaching positions: You work nine months and then have a nice long vacation (or hiatus, as they say in the Biz.) *Dallas* staff writers get one week off at Christmas, and even the cast works six days a week except for a short break in April and May. (Blessedly, the work week pares down to 'only' five 12-to-17-hour days when they're off location.)

From the first of June through mid-August ('When they set records for the number of heat strokes per square mile,' laughs Duffy), everyone moves to Texas and films the bulk of summertime and exterior shots.

You may have noticed that range-riding scenes are largely replaced by dining-room confrontations as each 'Dallas' season progresses. That's because after the first twelve of a usual 30 annual episodes (half a dozen more shows per season than most other series), everyone hightails it back to four soundstages on the MGM lot – now the Lorimar Telepictures studio, thanks in part to the revenues from this one show – and they film mainly interiors.

Although there is a 'Southfork' at the J.M. J. Ranch at Hidden Hills, a gated suburb north of Los Angeles, the original Southfork was Box Ranch in Frisco, Texas. On-location interiors were shot at a private residence at Turtle Creek, Texas, later duplicated in its entirety on MGM Stage 23 at Culver City, California. After the pilot season, Southfork moved to the 164-acre Duncan Acres estate at Plano, Texas, which has since legally changed its name to Southfork – and charges $4 head for up to 300 tourists a day to peek inside. ('It's smaller than I imagined,' is the usual reaction.)

It costs almost a million dollars per episode to film *Dallas* – and the show adds about $2 million cash income each shooting season to the local economy. Texas is loyal to *Dallas*, and even though only Larry Hagman out of all the show's stars is a true Texan, *Dallas* has become loyal to Texas. But it took them a while to get used to it.

'The heat does begin to debilitate a little in the afternoon,' says Katzman. 'But you get used to it. It's not so bad for the crew, but for the actors, the problem of sweating becomes a very real one. They're constantly

changing shirts. The ladies are out there too long and
you know what happens to their hair. It takes its toll.'
Lorimar spends up to $7,000 a year in make-up alone,
and every costume has to be bought in duplicate.
Make-up call is at 5:30 a.m., and the final shots of the
day are seldom completed until past 6:30 in the
evening.

The cast had to learn to live with the weather, and
with local customs. *Dallas* historian Suzy Kalter likes
to tell the story of an early show, filmed on the Box
Ranch, during which Sue Ellen was supposed to make
an entrance riding into frame on her quarterhorse. The
local livestock contractor had provided a mount for
actress Linda Gray – but ranch owner Cloyce Box
whispered to Leonard Katzman that a woman of Sue
Ellen's wealth wouldn't be caught dead riding an
animal of such mediocre quality. Box led in his own
$250,000 mare, and Gray completed the scene in
appropriate style.

The plot of each *Dallas* season is mapped out in
chunks, the first chunk of about twelve hours' worth
determined the day after wrapping the final episode of
the previous year. Creating by committee – under the
supervision of Katzman and Phil Capice – the writing
team orally interweaves numerous subplot outlines,
and usually has the drift down firmly enough by
around November to know what cliffhanger they're
heading toward. It takes about two weeks of intense
work at the typewriter to complete a single 52-page
script – for which a Writers' Guild member earns
approximately $16,000.

The first draft of each script – called a 'red cover'

because of its traditional binder, and stamped with enough high-security warnings to pass for a Pentagon position paper – is subject to change as the season unfolds. *Dallas* reality is suceptible to the exigencies of *real* reality: An ailing star needs to be written around or even out; the possibility of a SAG strike has to be provided for; or, perhaps most importantly, a character is increasing in popularity and his or her part has to be beefed up.

In the first full year of the show – now committed to serial form, after a token resistance with the first 10 new-season episodes – this is what happened to J.R. Says Duffy, 'When J.R. started getting all the attention, at first I went "Wait a minute, what's going on?" Now, it's perfectly fine with me. I am the first to admit that if it were not for the character of J.R., the show would not be successful. If I were producing *Dallas*, my choices wouldn't have been the choices made. And we would have failed in the second year.'

To continue the story of the Ewings as it unfolded during the first year of *Dallas*:

When Bobby runs into his ne'er-do-well brother Gary in Las Vegas, he naturally urges him to come home to Southfork. Unbeknownst to either, the young terror Lucy Ewing has been visiting Gary's estranged wife – her mother, Valene – and Lucy tries to reunite the couple. This distresses J.R., who fears that Gary might butt into Ewing Oil business. J.R., after all, was the one who originally broke them up: threatened Val's life, and stole her daughter.

While J.R. sets up his own brother for a fall, Digger

Barnes comes onto the scene, and disowns his daughter for marrying a Ewing. Pam has more unhappiness in store: When Bobby's ex-love, Jenna Wade, returns to Dallas with a 7-year-old daughter who just might be Bobby's child, J.R. uses them both as a wedge between Pam and her husband.

Bobby chooses his wife – and he chooses peace of mind over the Ewing fortune. When J.R. reacts to his father's heart attack by making deals based on the assumption that he's about to inherit the firm, Bobby decides he'd rather leave Texas than turn into a man like his big brother.

As Sue Ellen tries to buy herself a first-born for $15,000, J.R. threatens Pam with accusations of bigamy stemming from a youthful marriage that had been annulled. Bobby saves Lucy from a kidnapper, and Pam is torn between supporting her brother Cliff in his run for the state senate and siding with her new family, who of course oppose him. J.R. ruins Cliff's campaign by smearing him for past sexual indiscretions, and Pam swears to her brother-in-law: 'Someday... you're going to pay for what you did....'

The rascal J.R. redeems himself somewhat when he and Bobby are involved in a plane crash. As Miss Ellie worries that the news of their fate may topple Jock with another heart attack, J.R. saves the crash victims by his quickthinking – but not before a worried Sue Ellen has irretrievably hit the bottle. The drinking is partly responsible for her affair with hubby's arch-enemy Cliff Barnes, an affair that results in long-barren Sue Ellen's pregnancy. Even Sue Ellen herself isn't sure, though, whether the father is J.R. or Cliff.

While J.R. waits for his daddy to hurry up and die so that he can drill for oil on Digger Barnes's old grub-stake, Section 40 of Southfork, Bobby goes into the construction business. But before he can get it off the ground, he's taken away at gunpoint by kidnappers who think they've got J.R. With Cliff as a go-between, the kidnappers arrange a swap with J.R. – who tries, but fails, to turn it into a mix-up proving fatal for Cliff.

While Jock is recuperating and Sue Ellen is wavering between J.R., Cliff and the bottle, Miss Ellie receives a shock: Her brother Garrison, long thought dead, returns to Southfork. J.R. is terrified that he has come to claim his birthright – which Ellie would gladly hand over to him – but he has only come home to die. Jock, feeling old, strikes up a friendship with J.R.'s former flame Julie Grey, and J.R. naturally tells his mama all about it. He also sets Julie up as a corporate spy, pushes her into the arms of Cliff Barnes and – possibly – off the roof of her home. He then frames Cliff for her death.

While Bobby sincerely tries to help Cliff out of the jam J.R. has arranged for him, Pam moves out in anger over the repercussions of this never-ending feud. Bobby discovers the evidence that exonerates both Cliff and J.R. of the killing, and begs his wife to return: 'Pam, you knew I was a Ewing when you married me, and I'm going to be a Ewing until I die . . . I love you and I want you back.'

With both J.R. and Cliff rooting for a split between Bobby and Pam, Sue Ellen's sister, Kristin, becomes the new pawn in their game. Both men encourage her interest in Bobby, while J.R. traps Pam in a compromising photograph that is splashed all over the local paper

– effectively ruining both her reputation and Cliff's political chances. Meanwhile, Lucy has fallen in love with Kit Mainwaring III, who turns out to be gay. With Bobby's help, the couple cancel their marriage plans without damaging the family honour.

Now, Ray Krebbs falls in love with Donna McCullum – who happens to be married to ex-governor Sam Culver, a powerful ally of J.R. Before J.R. can blackmail Donna into increasing his power base, she leaves Sam for Ray, much to the joy of both Pam and Bobby, neither of whom want to see Ray hurt again.

Sue Ellen, despite the risk to her pregnancy, falls deeper into alcohol addition. J.R. institutionalizes her against her will, and she tearfully tells Bobby of her love for Cliff . . . and the likelihood that he's the father of her baby. When she sees a picture of Cliff with another woman, she drunkely attempts an escape from the sanitarium. Her mad flight culminates in an auto accident, and Sue Ellen is rushed to Dallas Memorial Hospital for emergency surgery to save the life of her baby.

As the year comes to an end, the prematurely born John Ross Ewing III is barely clinging to life. 'Will he live?' a distraught Cliff Barnes asks his sister Pam. 'They don't know.'

Year One of *Dallas* crossed the line between series and serial somewhere about a third of the way through the season. And while some involved in the production brag that it was the first big-budget nighttime soap opera and the virtual inventor of the cliffhanger, that's not strictly true.

One of the reasons *Dallas* became so successful with

this format is that the very idea of serials and cliff-hangers was already so well established and so welcomed by audiences.

Psychologists even have a name for the soap opera format: 'postponing closure.' As Dr Joyce Brothers explained, 'Storytellers as far back as Homer masterminded it; Charles Dickens used it so well that people queued up and waited for hours for monthly installments of his novels.' The cliffhanger itself was named more than fifty years ago, when moviemakers filled cinemas on Saturday mornings with 'The Perils of Pauline' and its ilk – and left the hero or heroine literally dangling off the end of the cliff at the end of each segment. Will he/she survive? Come back next week. . . .

Prime-time soap operas were the rage in Britain in the early '70s (*The Forsyte Saga*, *Poldark*, *Upstairs, Downstairs*) and even had a good run in America with the evening version of *Peyton Place*. And while Lorimar resisted a serialized format at first because it could cost them big dollars later on the syndication market, they were now commanding $350,000 per commercial minute as a ratings winner – and that ain't hay.

There was nothing really new about what *Dallas* was doing. They were just doing it better. 'I wasn't prepared for the way it caught on,' said Duffy. *Dallas* became an international *cause celebre*. South African television banned the episode dealing with Kit Mainwaring's homosexuality, because it offended the moral sensibilities of the government – which forced several newspapers there to print a detailed synopsis of the missing show. Strangers would come up to Patrick in the supermarket and commiserate with him about his wife's defection . . . 'and it took me a minute to realize they were talking about Pam, not Carlyn.'

What worked for *Dallas* was the very thing Leonard Katzman had stressed from the start, the idea David Jacobs had in the first place: the key word is 'family.' 'It is, oddly enough, a family show,' says Katzman, sex and scandal notwithstanding. 'Families like to watch it because they can compare their family with the Ewing family – albeit their family is not as wealthy.' But they'd like to *imagine* they are, and that's all to the good. Says Larry Hagman: 'It's about business, it's about oil, it's about family relations, family loyalty – in essence, it promotes everything we've been taught to believe in in this country.'

Remember the opening of the classic Sixties hospital drama *Ben Casey*? It went: 'Man. Woman. Birth. Death. Infinity.' That pretty much sums up the things that really matter on *Dallas*. Man and woman – falling in love, making love, breaking up, cheating on each other, missing each other, finding each other, losing each other, deciding between each other and *another* other. Getting married, getting divorced, getting remarried. Birth – and pregnancy and abortion and miscarriage and adoption and (tastefully done, of course) conception itself. Death – in all its myriad forms, and sometimes its last-minute avoidance.

As to Infinity? Well, that's what we call 'length of contract.'

So as much as it become pivotal to the plot whether Gary Ewing owned a percentage share of the oil company – what really counted was that stock's effect on his marriage to Val. A Cliff Barnes environmental-impact report on shopping mall construction at Southfork might mean millions of dollars lost or gained – but, more to the point, could instigate a dispute between Bobby and his wife, Bobby and his brother, Bobby and his mother. . . . Family relationships will always last in the heart and mind long after the chequebook balance is forgotten.

It's important to note that these fundamentals – the same elements that flesh out a Vital Statistics page in any local newspaper – are also the touchstones of tabloid journalism. (And don't those yellowed clippings of Birth Announcements and Marriage Banns live in family scrapbooks long after the front-page news is a dim memory?) So the reciprocal relationship between *Dallas* and the popular weeklies was both instant and mutually beneficial. The attention of the tabloid press to *Dallas* (and its soapy offspring) was very much a part of the show's snowballing success.

But there will be much more about that later.

In the meantime, we have Man, Woman, Birth, Death and the Ewings. And, again like newsprint, television drama is stronger when the news is bad news. Rocky marriages pull better ratings than happy ones: problem pregnancies are more interesting than uneventful ones; sudden, tragic death evinces more tears than peaceful expiration in one's sleep.

The Ewing family was believable because the cast and crew themselves became one big family. Even if Patrick joked that, at first, Bobby really only said a few permutations on two standard lines: 'That's all right, Mom, I'll take care of it' and 'Okay, Mom, I took care of it' – and often compared his character's panache to 'a three-day-old leaf of lettuce', he was still part of the team, the family. If J.R.'s growing importance lessened Duffy's dramatic impact – if people stopped him on the street to ask him about J.R. – it hadn't started to wear thin just yet. He would smilingly reply that he had it in his contract to punch out his big brother X number of times per season, and he grew to become Larry Hagman's best friend.

'Leonard Katzman and Larry Hagman are my family,' he says. 'A triumvirate of friendships.' Patrick also became buddies with Steve Kanaly; the two go on 'R&R (Rest and Recreation) trips together. And Patrick and Larry started a tradition of practical jokes and scene-stealing games (particularly at Victoria Principal's expense) that became legend.

That 'walking genius' (Patrick's words, although they have been echoed by everyone else in the cast) Leonard Katzman wove the characters together into the *Dallas* family. But it was casting director Ruth Conforte who picked those players who would make them come alive. The same Ruth Conforte who had given Patrick Duffy his big break when she reconsidered him for the title role in *Man From Atlantis*.

We told you her name would come up again.

Next: The Players.

7

The People Behind The People

JOHN ROSS 'J.R.' EWING, JR: Larry Hagman

Larry Hagman was born in 1931 in Fort Worth, Texas, and he was born to act. His mother, Mary Martin, was one of Broadway's most successful actresses (*Peter Pan*, *South Pacific*); his father, Ben Hagman, was a lawyer. Larry's parents divorced when he was 12, and he went to Los Angeles to live with his grandmother until her death; then he returned to his since-remarried mother.

Hagman had attended Bard College for only a year when he decided to follow his calling. After a theatrical debut in Dallas, he went to the New York City Center and appeared in Shakespeare's *Taming of the Shrew* – which, oddly, would become a pet project play of Patrick Duffy's some years later.

Larry moved to England to join his mother in the cast of *South Pacific*, and lived in London for five years. At that time, he joined the Air Force and worked in the military entertainment division. It was in

England that he met and married Swedish designer Maj Axelsson, at the end of 1955. Their children, Kristina Mary (called Heidi) and Preston, were born in 1958 and 1962 respectively.

The Hagmans moved back to New York, where Larry appeared in a series of Broadway and off-Broadway plays and then landed a two-and-a-half-year gig as a regular on the daytime soap opera *Edge of Night*. In 1965, he moved to Hollywood and won a starring prime-time role as the beleaguered astronaut in the fluffy Barbara Eden sitcom *I Dream of Jeannie* which ran for five years.

Feature films to his credit include *Fail Safe*, *The Group*, *Harry and Tonto*, *Mother, Jugs, and Speed*, *Superman* and *S.O.B.* It was in the landmark 1974 rock'n'roll movie *Stardust* that he first developed the character that would become J.R.: a drawling, conniving band manager whose attitude toward business was, 'The world is a jungle . . . and I'm the meanest mother . . . .ing ape out there.'

Larry is also known for his sense of humour, his implacable opposition to tobacco smoking, and his volunteer work on behalf of the mentally handicapped. Although rumours of his conversion to Buddhism – at Patrick Duffy's behest – are false, it is true that Hagman makes a practice of never speaking on Saturdays: 'It just a way of taking a day off,' he says. Ironically, he communicates voluntarily through the same notes and whistles that his best friend was forced to use 15 years ago. Also ironically, the Hagmans frequently vacation in Montana, and Larry kept a photo of himself with Patrick Duffy's parents outside The

Lounge in Boulder, long before he knew that the couple were 'related' to him.

Larry and Maj are still together, living in a Santa Fe-style house at the Malibu Colony, where they particularly enjoy relaxing in their hot tub.

Remember the hot tub.

ELEANOR SOUTHWORTH EWING FARLOW:
Barbara Bel Geddes

The matriarch of the Ewing clan, born in 1922, also claims roots in the entertainment world; her father was the prominent stage designer Norman Bel Geddes. Her acting career began when she was still in her teens, making her New York stage debut in the comedy *Out of the Frying Pan*. During World War II she toured with the USO, then returned to a successful Broadway career.

Her acclaimed stage performances included starring roles in *The Moon Is Blue*, *Cat on a Hot Tin Roof*, *Mary, Mary* and *Luv*. She won the Clarence Derwent Award for Outstanding Young Actress of the Year when she co-starred in Elia Kazan's controversial *Deep Are the Roots*, a story of interracial love.

Bel Geddes moved to Hollywood to star opposite Henry Fonda in *The Long Night*, and received an Oscar nomination for her role in *I Remember Mama*. She is most often seen on late-show reruns of her sole musical performance, opposite Danny Kaye in *The Five Pennies*, and as James Stewart's long-suffering best girl in the Hitchcock classic *Vertigo*.

It was again with Hitchcock that she acheived cult

status on the small screen, in the Golden Age of Television's comedy-drama *Lamb to the Slaughter*. That was our Miss Ellie as the soft-spoken housewife who bashed her husband's brains in with a frozen leg of lamb – and then calmly fed the roasted evidence to investigating police officers.

Aside from her acting career, Bel Geddes is a writer and illustrator of children's books, having two to her credit: *I Like to Be Me* and *So Do I*. She also paints and designs stationery and greeting cards.

Barbara is the widow of Windsor Lewis and mother of two daughters, Susan and Betsy. She divides her times between her homes in quiet Putnam Valley, New York and a second residence at Marina del Rey, California. She is the only star of *Dallas* to have earned an Emmy, for her work on the show.

JOHN ROSS 'JOCK' EWING: Jim Davis

The late Jim Davis brought larger-than-life Jock Ewing to the screen, until Davis's death of cancer in 1981 (at the age of 64) felled both of them.

At 6' 3" and 13½ stone, with weathered features and a bold carriage, Davis was the quintessential Texan – although he was actually born in Missouri. His film career, though, leaned heavily toward classic Westerns, including *The Fabulous Texan*, *Red Stallion in the Rockies*, *Comes a Horseman* and *The Trackers*. Altogether, Davis appeared in more than 150 movies and some 300 television shows during his career.

After his graduation from William Jewel College in Liberty, Missouri, Davis joined a travelling circus, and later became a travelling salesman for (what else?) an oil company. It was after the firm transferred him to Los Angeles that he decided to pursue an acting career, and was hired by movie mogul Louis B. Mayer following a screen test with swimming star Esther Williams. Having completed a number of co-starring roles, he joined the Navy in World War II, and later returned to Hollywood.

More recent films to Davis's credit include *Parallax View*, with Warren Beatty, and the acclaimed made-for-TV movie *Just A Little Inconvenience*. Jim's widow, Blanche, still occupies the comfortable family home in suburban Northridge, California.

PAMELA BARNES EWING: Victoria Principal
Victoria (never call her Vicky) Principal was born in Japan in 1950 (or thereabouts), the daughter of an Italian-American Army Air Force Sergeant-Major, Victor Principal, and his British wife, Ree Veal (yes, really!)

The 'Army brat' moved around a great deal in her childhood, and a posting in England enabled her to attend the prestigious Royal Academy of Dramatic Arts at the tender age of five. But it was only when the family was posted to Miami, Florida that Victoria stayed put long enough to seriously pursue her interest in acting. She took drama lessons there – and studied to be a chiropractor at Miami-Dade Junior College, as well, just in case.

Lusciously dark and petite, Principal established herself as a model in Manhattan, and became romantically linked with an assortment of well-known and powerful men. She was a globetrotting jet-setter for a while, then moved to Los Angeles to launch a screen career.

Her major motion-picture debut was as Paul Newman's Mexican lover in *The Life and Times of Judge Roy Bean*. She had small roles in *I Will, I Will . . . for Now* with Elliott Gould and in the all-star *Earthquake*, and she undertook a controversial (because it was filmed, as the title indicates, *sans* clothing) role in *The Naked Ape*. She was featured in a *Playboy* magazine nude layout, and after that (although not necessarily because of it), her on-screen career fizzled.

But Principal was undaunted. She began a second career as an artists' agent, and excelled in her hobby as a stock car racing driver. She married actor Chris Skinner (they met when he had a guest spot on *Dallas*), later divorcing him and taking up with pop star Andy Gibb. Currently, she is contentedly married to plastic surgeon Dr Harry Glassman and stepmother to his two children.

Yet another career for Principal has utilized her personal flair for beauty and fitness to author self-help books offering advice on how others can mould themselves in a similar vein. *The Body Principal* and *The Beauty Principal* were well enough received that Victoria turned them into a trilogy with *The Diet Principal*.

SUE ELLEN SHEPARD EWING: Linda Gray
Linda Gray was born 1944-ish in the very Culver City area that now houses *Dallas* sound stages. An

admittedly awkward adolescent, Linda attended a strict Roman Catholic school, Notre Dame Academy, in Los Angeles, and didn't begin to blossom as a beauty until she graduated high school.

In her late teens, she began a top modelling career, and boasts more than 400 television commercials as well as a slew of print ads in her CV. It was during her years as a model that she met and married art director Ed Thrasher, from whom she has since been divorced.

Gray was 32 years old before she began to take the idea of an acting career seriously, and enrolled in professional drama classes. After a guest appearance on *Marcus Welby, M.D.*, she was cast by producer Norman Lear in the controversial comedy *All That Glitters*; she played a transsexual named Linda Murkland. That was her only regular series job until *Dallas*, but she also appeared in made-for-TV movies including *Murder in Peyton Place*, *The Grass is Greener Over the Septic Tank*, *The Two Worlds of Jennie Logan* and *Not in Front of the Children*. Her feature film credits include *Under the Yum Yum Tree*, *Palm Springs Weekend* and *Dogs*.

Although she did not receive the Emmy for which she was nominated in 1981, Gray was awarded its Italian equivalent, Il Gato, in 1982, and was named Woman of the Year by the Hollywood Radio and Television Society that same season.

And then there are the half-Ewings and Ewings-in-law and almost-Ewings and ex-Ewings and Ewings-in-waiting: Ken Kercheval (as Cliff Barnes), Steve Kanaly (Ray Krebbs), Susan Howard (Donna Culver Krebbs),

Charlene Tilton (Lucy Ewing Cooper), Leigh McCloskey (Mitch Cooper), Audrey Landers (Afton Cooper), Ted Shackelford (Gary Ewing), Joan Van Ark (Valene Ewing), Dack Rambo (Jack Ewing), Jenilee Harrison (Jamie Ewing), Howard Keel (Clayton Farlow), Jared Martin (Dusty Farlow), Mary Crosby (Kristin Shepard), Priscilla Presley (Jenna Wade), John Beck (Mark Graison), Priscilla Pointer (Rebecca Wentworth), Morgan Brittany (Katherine Wentworth), Tina Louise (Julie Grey), Lois Chiles (Holly Harwood), Deborah Shelton (Mandy Winger) . . . the list goes on. A few more seasons – currently, ratings prognosticators say *Dallas* has a good three years to go, which happens to be the length of Patrick Duffy's latest contract – and we may as well just photocopy the SAG directory for this section. But, hey, without each and every one of them, those *Dallas* nights we wait for would be filled with strangers.

8

Why Shoot J.R.?

We pick up the Ewing saga now at the beginning of the second year of Dallas:

As a depressed Sue Ellen refuses to see her miracle baby, and J.R. and Cliff fight over its paternity, John Ross III is kidnapped. Pam saves the child, only to learn from Digger that the baby – and any child she might have – could inherit the Barnes fatal, genetic disease. And now Pam herself is pregnant.

Sue Ellen's sister, Kristin, begins making a play for J.R., and a wounded Jock reveals to his eldest son the secret of his marriage to Amanda. Sue Ellen begins an affair with rodeo star Dusty Farlow; Miss Ellie is afraid to tell Jock that she has breast cancer; and Pam loses Bobby's second unborn baby.

Ellie, devastated by her mastectomy, finally allows oil rigs on Southfork land – a move necessitated by J.R.'s overambitious speculations. Pam acts as mother to Sue Ellen's unaccepted child, and weeps when Sue Ellen finally acknowledges the boy.

Gary and Val decide to remarry; J.R. is unable to

rush home in time to stop them. He instead sees to it that Pam's workload increases so that she is ever more distant from Bobby, and brings Bobby back to Ewing Oil rather than let Jock regain command.

Digger Barnes spills the news about Cliff's paternity of John Ross III, which isn't welcomed by the newly paired couple Sue Ellen and Dusty. Finally, a blood test proves that J.R. was the father all along. Nor does Bobby appear to be the father of Jenna Wade's Charlie – it's Renaldo Marchetta, the scoundrel she married. But Jenna is determined to get Bobby back anyway.

Both Ewing couples – J.R. and Sue Ellen, Bobby and Pam – are on the brink of divorce. Both decide that family is paramount, and try to work it out one more time; however, for Sue Ellen this is a play to get sole custody of John Ross. J.R., of course, wins this fight through his usual foul means. And Dusty Farlow is presumed killed in a plane crash.

A most dramatic development come when the new assistant district attorney, Cliff Barnes, arrests Jock for the 30-year-old murder of ranch hand Hutch McKinney. The solution, eventually, is both sad and relieving for Pam: On his death-bed, Digger Barnes confesses to the crime. Hutch was having an affair with Pam's mother, which is why Digger shot him. And Hutch is Pam's biological father, which means she can have a healthy baby after all.

Miss Ellie sets out to find Amanda, Jock's first wife, and Pam sets out to find her own mother, long presumed dead. Meanwhile, J.R. has a field day in the oil fields, setting up a massive deal based on inside information – a deal that makes him even wealthier, and ruins many of his colleagues. Cliff Barnes finds proof that Digger owned half of Ewing Oil. J.R. threatens Sue Ellen with institutionalization. Pam and Bobby leave Southfork in disgust. J.R. sets up Kristin for arrest on prostitution charges.

And as J.R. Ewing is working late in his office, an unknown intruder shoots him at point-blank range.

The 21 March 1980 episode of *Dallas* was the most watched series television show of the year. Some 40 million Americans and 300 million viewers in 57 other countries watched J.R. get it, and the show was almost singlehandedly responsible for the CBS network's first ratings leadership in three years. More than half the British population stayed home to watch the show; highways were emptied. The BBC ran the shooting as a top news story; British bookmakers accepted bets on the culprit's identity (Dusty Farlow was a 6–4 favourite).

Half a dozen 'J.R.' novelty songs hit the radio airwaves; millions of buttons and bumper stickers read 'I Shot J.R.' (Lorimar earned more than $100,000 in merchandising royalties from buttons alone). Ronald Reagan printed up signs saying, 'A Democrat Shot J.R.,' and presidential candidate Jimmy Carter came to Dallas on a fundraising tour claiming that he had scheduled the trip only to find out whodunnit.

Larry Hagman was offered £100,000 cash in London for spilling the beans – but Hagman had no idea who the guilty party was himself. Neither did Patrick Duffy, or any of the cast, for that matter. Only about 15 people knew who shot J.R.: *Dallas* producers, story editors, a couple of executives at Lorimar and CBS. They swore not to tell even their immediate families. The actors were among the last to know, since almost all of them were filmed at one time or another with a smoking gun in their hand; they watched the solution on 21 November (postponed from 19 September) along with 350 million other curious viewers.

The main reason nobody knew who had shot J.R. was that no one knew who *was going* to shoot J.R. The entire plot development was a last-minute addition to a season that was supposed to end with Digger Barnes's death. When CBS ordered two more hours of programming, Phil Capice said 'Let's have J.R. get his.' As Leonard Katzman recalled, 'we said, "Let's shoot him and figure out who did it later."'

There were more plot reasons for the shooting of J.R. than Kristin Shepard's venom (Yes, she did it, just as Jimmy the Greek predicted). Patrick Duffy said in 1980, 'The reason J.R. was shot was to put me in a position to take over Ewing Oil.' It was time to give Bobby Ewing a little more depth; to pursue, as Duffy called it, 'the corruption of an honest man.'

'It's tough to write for the good guy,' says Patrick. 'Bobby got the short end of the stick. Now, he could get tougher. Be more of a realist. Do things a little off-centre in terms of legalities – as long as the people on the negative side deserve it, and the right people are going to benefit from it.

'We're trying to broaden him.'

And then there was the *real* reality underlying the plot reality, as well. At this time, Larry Hagman was holding out for more money in a contract renegotiation.

In fact, the early episodes of the following season, with
J.R. hospitalized and at the brink of death, were filmed
with a stand-in – Hagman himself was out of the
country. The threats cut both ways: 'Give me what I
want or do without J.R.' on one side, and "Accept our
offer or we let J.R. die' on the other. It was a game of
flinch.

'We were all going, "Hang in there, Larry! You
deserve what you get,"' says Duffy. 'When he got what
he wanted, we all went "All right!" His greatest rooting
section was all of us in the cast. We didn't all of a
sudden give him a higher chair, but we acknowledged
his importance after the holdout.' The precedent proved applicable to Patrick later on.

After the 'Who Shot J.R.' phenomenon, *Dallas*
became both an immovable object and an irresistible
force. It begat *Knots Landing, Dynasty, The Colbys,
Falcon Crest* and a few others less successful. It went
into syndication in 112 markets, promoted by a
$500,000 series of teaser spots explaining the plot so
far. Even people who knew who shot J.R., it seemed,
still wanted to watch it happen all over again. Walk-on
parts in the show were raffled off for $225 a chance at a
charity fundraiser. A line of Southfork fashions and
Southfork colognes, a J.R. board game and desk set,
and a *Dallas* comic book were put into development.
Work began on *Dallas: The Movie* and *Dallas: The
Record*. There was even talk of a *Dallas* line of frozen
foods.

Turkey's national parliament cut short its session so
that elected officials could make it home in time for the
show.

'You can't tell what's real and not real in all these stories,' Larry Hagman said at the beginning of *Dallas: The Early Years*. (The three-hour-long, made-for-TV movie was finally completed in 1986.) And that's what happened with *Dallas* itself, and its massive influence on the viewing public. Reality and plot became confused – or, at any rate, equally important.

'I was on location once, in the mansion at Turtle Creek,' recalls Hagman, 'and an old lady came up to me. Really slow. With a walker. I knew she was going to ask for my autograph, so I smiled. She took her purse – she had a little purse – and hit me right above the ear with it! I saw stars. Turned out she had a Smith and Wesson .38 in there, that her late husband had given her for protection 10 years ago. She forgot she had it. "I'm sorry," she said, "but you *are* a rascal."'

Although Patrick says 'I don't take Bobby home with me,' he also acknowledges that 'he's a friend.' And keeping up Bobby's Boy Scout image has impacted on Patrick's real life. For instance, he stopped drinking in public – which gave rise to the rumours that he was a teetotaller. This tied in nicely with the media exploitation of his religious philosophies, although his devotion to Buddhism is quite real and had not been exaggerated. In fact, Patrick generally spent his Friday nights at NSA meetings, while the rest of the country was in front of the tube watching Bobby.

'I had to start building an identity apart from the show,' said Patrick. But that wouldn't prove to be easy, because as he himself noted, *Dallas* is a self-motivating press machine.'

That 'man, woman, birth, death, infinity' soap-opera foundation is also the lifeblood of the popular tabloids. The only difference between broadcast and print media is in the definition of 'infinity': the *National Enquirer*, the *Star* and their less-thorough cousins have developed an appropriate sub-genre for it that includes life after death, UFOs, and miracle anti-wrinkle treatments. The best cover story you can hope for, though (and this applies to glossier publications like *People* and *Us*, too) is some nice juicy gossip about a Household Name – preferably a love affair, marriage, divorce, pregnancy, childbirth, illness or death.

The path to Household Name status is similar to that for becoming royalty. (Come to think of it, *being* royalty will do the trick.) You're born into it, or you marry into it. The other way to become a Household Name is to do something that will make you instantly recognizable to more than 10 million strangers. Outside of committing high crimes and misdemeanors or seeking national office, the likeliest way to achieve that is getting on a prime-time TV series.

Patrick Duffy – and everyone else on *Dallas* – earned that often unwelcome Household Name status the day the show first cracked the Neilsen top 10. Their wives retroactively married into it; their children were retroactively born into it. And when it comes to a good headline, the editors don't really mind whether the story is about 'Bobby' or 'Patrick,' 'Larry' or 'J.R.' As long as nine out of ten people in the supermarket check-out queue can identify the picture without reading the caption, the subject qualifies.

'In the beginning, the relationship between *Dallas* and the tabloids was completely adversarial,' recalls *National Enquirer* reporter Sam Rubin. 'They were desperate not to let the secrets out to us, and we were equally desperate to get them. We wouldn't do anything against the law, but, boy were we anxious to . . . ah, chat with crew members, cast members, anyone who might be privy to what was going on.

'To the "tabs", a cliffhanger is like the Democratic National Convention for a political reporter. We're all over them like a blanket.'

It became standard operating procedure to offer up to $5,000 – cash – for a pirated copy of a pivotal script. *Dallas* scripts were reputedly bound with a strip of metal inside the covers, to set off airport-style weapon detectors at the studio gates. 'Deep Throat' (as in Watergate, not Linda Lovelace) insiders were met in coffee shops, petrol stations, any place anonymous. . . . 'We felt like drug dealers,' said one reporter.

In time, the relationship became somewhat more friendly. Although Leonard Katzman denies to this day that there are any intentional leaks from *Dallas* to the tabs – aside from occasional disinformation – Rubin diagrees. 'it became clear to them that tabloid coverage was becoming a tremendous promotional vehicle,' says the likeable journalist. 'Even revealing the plot ahead of time didn't hurt the ratings. It actually helped: We may tell you what happens, but you have to watch the show to see *how* it happens.'

Another tabloid veteran notes 'It's gotten to the point now that the reporters doing this are quite well known to the producers, and it's not uncommon for us to receive anonymous phone calls offering scripts. It may not be a producer, but it may be a producer whispering to a secretary or a janitor or anyone who could use a few bucks, "Psst! Take this" . . .'

'It's a totally reciprocal relationship,' says Rubin. 'And a guy like Patrick Duffy benefitted enormously from tabloid coverage.'

Problem was, Patrick Duffy just didn't live a tabloid kind of life. 'I'm a pretty boring person in terms of what they find interesting,' says Patrick. 'I hardly go out, so there's little opportunity to catch me anywhere. I seldom go to restaurants – but neither am I a sensational recluse. What are they going to do – send someone with a long lens to catch me mowing my lawn?

The only thing they thought was interesting was when they printed about my being a Buddhist. And then everyone went, "So what?" and that was that.'

'There's nothing really juicy about Duffy, nothing trashy. You're not talking about Joan Collins, here,' says one of L.A.'s hot paparazzi. 'I remember being assigned to him once, and got all excited when he drove out to Hollywood instead of heading home to the Valley. He pulled into this building on Santa Monica Boulevard – not the classiest part of town – and I'm licking my lips. Turns out the guy's taking *dancing class*, and this was the studio!'

The Duffys steadfastly refused to be 'good ink'. They continued to live in their $170,000, one-storey, five-bedroom house in a better section of the San Fernando Valley – but not so 'better' that they required a guard house or a stone wall. Instead, the front of the modest-looking residence is a gentle, ivy-covered slope. There is a metal gate, but the Duffy boys could easily scale it themselves. Patrick and Carlyn bought the three-bedroom home next door for their guest house, and Patrick happily drove to local shops in his 1980 Jeep.

They put in a pool – and maintained it themselves with the assistance of their sons. Okay, the family developed a tatse for caviar, and Patrick did once hire a limousine to take his younger son to a Beverly Hills birthday party. Still, that hardly qualifies for *Lifestyles of the Rich and Famous*.

But that didn't stop England's *News of the World* from printing that Patrick lives in 'a four million-pound, 30-room mansion ... complete with Mercedes.' Or *Star* from saying that he bought a 'magnificent mansion outside Nashville, Tennessee, that is almost a carbon copy of the Ewing family home.' If there's no story, and the readers want a story... a story will be found.

So it made headlines when the Duffy housekeeper 'revealed' that Carlyn spent $700 on cosmetics. The 'short-tempered' woman was going on 'extravagant shopping sprees' because 'she seems to be worried about her age and appearance. She knows she's 10 years older than her husband!'

How could she not know?

Then, the same publication will happily announce that the Duffys' steadfast union has saved Patrick's soul; that the strain of the series almost ruined him, until his wife showed him the value of home and hearth: 'Love Saves Patrick Duffy's Marriage – After "Dallas" Nearly Destroyed It', the headline read.

When Patrick was absent on the day of the annual

Actor turns camera man at the opening day of *Captain E.O.* at Disneyland, Los Angeles, 1986.
Frank Edwards/Fotos International

Duffy with his wife Carlyn and son Patrick at a celebrity sports special in Malibu, 1977.
Frank Edwards/Fotos International

The young star of *Man from Atlantis* at the NBC Affiliate Convention in Los Angeles, 1977.
Frank Edwards/Fotos International

Sporting his beard grown for his role in *The Taming of the Shrew* at a Hollywood Foreign Press Association brunch, 1982. *Frank Edwards/Fotos International*

A far cry from Bobby: in *The Taming of the Shrew* at Hofstra University, New York, 1982. *Star File*

In addition to playing Bobby Ewing, Patrick has
directed several episodes of *Dallas* (1983).
Russell C. Turiak

Duffy in a scene from *Enola Gay* (1980) with Robert Pine (right) and Billy Crystal, to his left.
Globe Photos

Besieged by reporters at Heathrow Airport on the way to filming *Strong Medicine* with Dick Van Dyke and Pamela Sue Martin, 1985. At the time speculation was rife about Bobby's rumoured return to *Dallas. Globe Photos*

Patrick and Carlyn at a party for producer Glenn Larson at Chasens Restaurant in Los Angeles, 1985.
Greg De Guire/Celebrity Photos

The urban cowboy at a taping of *Martin Luther King, Jr: A Celebration of Life* in Washington, DC, 1984. *Stan Young/Galella Ltd*

Larry Hagman as J.R. Ewing, welcomes Patrick Duffy back to the cast of *Dallas*, 1986. *Globe Photos*

Duffy as Bobby Ewing and Priscilla Presley as Jenna Wade enjoy a dance at a ball in *Dallas*, 1986. *Globe Photos*

Bobby finds his new love in *Dallas* in the autumn of 1987. Lisa Alden, played by Amy Stock, engineers a meeting on ice where Bobby is skating with his son Christopher. *Russell C. Turiak*

cast photo shoot, tabloid headlines screamed, 'Bitter Real-Life Feud Erupts on Dallas Set!' and 'Patrick Duffy Loses Halo' and 'Dallas Cast Snubs Patrick Duffy.' *USA Today* reported that Patrick had 'received a message from heaven that warned him not to attend the photo session.' Actually, he was tied up in an editing room on a pressing film project.

Patrick takes it all with a shrug; 'journalistic license,' he calls it.

'Patrick knows how to handle the press,' says Rubin. 'He does the circuit: talk shows, music award shows, specials. He's out there.'

The one thing that you read in the gossip pages about the goings on at the *Dallas* set which do, in fact, reflect the truth are the tales of practical jokes. Someone really did put a lizard in Larry Hagman's lizardskin briefcase. And Hagman did try to spend money with his own picture on the notes. Our personal favourite: The time Bobby was due to save the day (yet again) in the script, this time by pulling an unconscious Sue Ellen from her disabled car. With the cameras rolling, Patrick came onto the scene and, totally departing from directorial expectation, tore off his shirt to reveal a complete red-and-blue costume underneath. 'This is a job for Superman!' he cried, and the crew laughed uncontrollably as he attempted to lift Linda Gray over his head and fly away with her.

9

Untapped Reserves

We go back now to the Ewings as J.R. languishes in hospital after escaping death from his gunshot wound.

An incapacitated J.R. gives his little brother new room to stretch. Bobby adapts easily to power, suceeding in a business coup even Jock had never managed – buying an oil refinery. J.R. does everything he can to mess up Bobby's deals behind his back, of course, even from his hospital bed. But even when Bobby, eventually, leaves Southfork and sets up an alternative energy company, he did quite well on his own. His marriage may be splitting at the seams, thanks to the pressures of his job and Pam's at The Store, but business-wise he is steamrolling right along.

Bobby wins election as State Senator for Texas's 33rd District, and uses his newfound political clout to establish a wildlife preserve. He and Pam adopt the baby Kristin Shepard bore just before she died, naming him Christopher after his mother and raising him as their own. To save the baby for Pam, Bobby gives up 20 voting shares of Ewing Oil to J.R. – and even with that handicap, wins out over J.R. in a desperate power struggle that Jock had arranged for his two sons to ensure that control of the company would go to the better man.

When actor Jim Davis's untimely death made it necessary for Jock Ewing to write his will onscreen, the senior Ewing left equal portions of the family business to each boy – with a 'winner take all' clause rewarding the half-owner whose share proved most profitable.

The battle between Bobby and J.R. over control of Ewing Oil rings the death knell for the once-solid marriage between Bobby and Pam. Though he avoids the advances of Pam's half-sister, Katherine Wentworth, Katherine tricks Bobby into believing that Pam is having an affair with dashing Mark Graison. Pam tells her husband that she can no longer go on living at Southfork, and he tells her that, with his family in a shambles, he can't leave.

'You are going to have to choose between me and Ewing Oil,' says Pam. 'You cannot have us both.' In 1983, Pam and Bobby Ewing are divorced.

Pam falls into the arms of Graison, and Bobby falls into the arms of his childhood sweetheart, Jenna Wade. But Katherine isn't about to take no for an answer: Rather than see Bobby marry Jenna, she shoots him in the back. Bobby is temporarily blinded, and only avoids being killed thanks to the intervention of (amazingly) J.R. On the verge of marrying Jenna, Bobby watches in horror as Jenna is kidnapped by her ex-husband, and then arrested for murdering her attacker.

Much as he and Pam still love each other, Bobby can't leave Jenna in her time of need. And Pam has promised to marry Graison. . . .

The problem with all this, though, was that Patrick Duffy as an actor was becoming 'lazy,' as he puts it. 'Once you've established a character, you don't re-establish that character in every scene for six years. I don't know too many people on *Dallas* who go home with the script of an important scene, and wonder how their character would play this scene. I don't worry about how Bobby would play a scene; I know instinctively.

'I've become lazy by virtue of not having to go home and construct a character. Most television actors are lazy – they work harder than anybody else because of the pace and what they have to do, but when you do television for a long time, it becomes habitual.'

The first thing that gave Duffy a chance to spread his own wings, much the way he insisted that Bobby be given a chance to spread his, was an opportunity, during the third season, to direct three episodes of the show. He would continue directing at least that many segments in each year to follow (with one notable exception). Not only did it give him new skills and new professional aspirations, but it gave him another $22,000 director's salary per show.

'Anyone in my position can hold their breath until they faint, and then their lawyers will go out and negotiate a directorial debut for them,' he laughs. 'I want to get to the point where I will go out and direct other things besides *Dallas*. You can't really only direct within your own show and have the outside world accredit you with being a director.'

As he told *TV Guide* in 1981, directing quickly became a professional obsession. 'I'm concentrating on other parts of my career,' he said. 'Acting in *Dallas* is now an enjoyable income tool.' Besides, he later joked, directing 'gives me something to think about while I'm acting!'

But on the serious side, practicing this new craft gave Patrick a respect for his own directors that he had never before felt in quite this degree. It no doubt further endeared him to them, as well. And it also gave him a new appreciation for his acting colleagues, getting an objective view of exactly what was demanded of them on a daily basis. In all, decided Patrick, 'directing is the most satisfying thing I've attempted so far.'

He also tried to land different, more challenging acting jobs during the brief *Dallas* hiatus, but found this task more difficult than he had assumed. 'No one wanted to hire me to be a guest star on a show that already had a sex symbol as a star,' he told writer Curt Davis. Being a hunk, he discovered, was a pain. 'If you're considered that attractive a public personage, they tend to lessen your capabilities, they don't give you the parameters to expand that they would give some other person who has this reputation as a great actor.'

He did get to appear in a two-part episode of *Charlie's Angels* – happily, its existing sex symbols were all female – and starred in a special made-for-TV movie called *Enola Gay*, playing the pilot of the plane which dropped the atomic bomb on Hiroshima. He also co-starred with Brian Keith, Lawrence Pressman and Cindy Pickett in *Cry for the Strangers*, a TV movie he jokingly referred to later as 'Cry for the Audience.'

One of the more noble roles he landed during a *Dallas* hiatus was in 1982, when he starred as Petruccio in a Hofstra University production of *Taming of the Shrew* at the John Cranford Adams Playhouse – following, interestingly, in Larry Hagman's footsteps. He grew a beard for the part, but was still identified in everyone's mind as good ol' Bobby; few in the audience realized until they read their programmes that Patrick had trained with the Old Globe. 'I'm sure they wondered about whether I could hold my own,' said Duffy.

The cast was equally dubious about Patrick's pretentions to *real* acting ability: 'I mean, there's nothing that says a television cowboy is going to be able to cut Shakesepare. I think that, at first, everybody was kind of standing around saying, "Okay, let's see ..."'

The production was well-received. And then Patrick proved himself more than adequate in an entirely different area, when he recorded the duet 'Together We're Strong' with French pop star Mirielle Mathieu. 'I don't really sing, but I can belt out a song,' he had once said, but he was obviously being too modest. The single went Top Ten in Europe, and eventually sold to platinum status. He made a music video with Mathieu, which he found amusing as she was no taller than Charlene Tilton. Patrick always towered over his female co-stars, which has made him very adept at bending at the knees for close-ups.

American record companies approached him about making a country & western album, which would have sold easily in the US thanks to his popularity as Bobby, but he declined. 'I've no intention of pursuing a singing career,' he told *Screen International*, despite tabloid headlines to the contrary.

'I had to shoot a layout for *Paris Match* magazine to promote that record,' remembers photographer Russell Turiak. 'Duffy was heading to Paris for a top TV show over there, and was going to sing on the show. I never did get to hear him sing.

'But he was wonderful to work with on the magazine shoot. He had already directed 13 episodes of *Dallas* at that time, he told me, and he really played "director" with me – took part in the process, gave suggestions, came up with some good ideas. He was professional, cooperative, easy to deal with. Never made it tough.'

In 1980, Patrick followed in his character's political footsteps when he was elected to the board of the Screen Actors' Guild, running on an actors' rights ticket. 'I have a moral obligation to assume responsibility for our growth in the future,' he told the *Daily News*, and that echoes his basic Buddhist philosophy: 'We each have total responsibility for our own lives.'

Patrick's biggest creative stretch, however, was in 1983 when he became the star and co-executive producer of his first feature film, *Vamping*. Filmed for less than $1 million (industry average for a feature is $7 million) on a 40-day shooting schedule in and around Buffalo, New York, *Vamping* cast Patrick as down-on-his-luck saxophonist Harry Baranski. Patrick took guild minimum wages for his participation, and studied religiously with sax player Bobby Militello for his onstage scenes. 'I think I pulled it off – even with Kleenex stuffed up my horn!' he laughs.

Duffy wanted to do the scruffy, unsympathetic lead in *Vamping* mainly because it was such a new departure for him. 'As a result of *Dallas*,' he says, 'I'm offered concerned, handsome young leading man good-guy roles. Lots of spouseless fathers, very vogue since *Kramer vs. Kramer.*

'*Vamping* is the opposite. Harry really gets it – and deserves what he gets. He's a slob, on the skids. Very self-destructive. He steals a piece of evidence in a murder case. This isn't *Man With A Horn* – it's a Hitchock-type, hunt-and-chase story that happens to involve a musician.'

Out of support for the concept of independent filmmaking, Patrick accepted only the minimum allowable salary for his work, plus a percentage of the profits ('points') should the picture do well. 'I got a part that I probably wouldn't be offered in this town for a good number of years, because it was atypical of the characters I tended to play,' he says. 'They were very happy to have me because of *Dallas*. I can sell that film in places where it cannot be sold.'

Unfortunately, *Vamping* didn't live up to the filmmakers' commercial expectations. 'The movie didn't really take off,' said one of the project publicists. 'It opened regionally' . . . but not until almost two years after it was completed. 'It was very offbeat,' says the publicist, who remembers the filming itself to have been 'very cold, up there in Buffalo,' but recalls Patrick as having been 'one of the most pleasant people I've ever worked with.'

Vamping is now available on videocassette, and is occasionally broadcast on outlets like USA cable. Those who are able to find it will be amazed that the first words out of Duffy's mouth on screen are 'Oh, shit.' Imagine the shock, hearing Bobby Ewing use 'the F word,' or seeing him exposing his bare bum to the camera! Harry Baranski really is a nasty piece of work. Obsessed by a woman he knows to be involved in a murder plot, he descends into a spiral of emotional corruption until there is no way out.

Vamping wasn't a bad movie. The production values betray its low budget, and the plot is somewhat predictable until a neat twist at the end. But the biggest problem is exactly the one Patrick wanted to overcome: how can we viewers, used to the clean-cut, upright Bobby Ewing, accept Patrick Duffy as this foul-mouthed, dishonest down-and-outer? Even through the stubble and underneath the soiled cap, Duffy always seems somehow . . . wholesome.

But Patrick was nonetheless glad he did the film. 'Harry Baranski is just about diametrically opposite to Bobby Ewing,' he said, and that was the most important thing.

Patrick Duffy proved in *Vamping* that he could be a not-so-goody-two-shoes. It's just too bad not very many people got to see him do it.

This project gave the actor/producer some new insights into his craft. For one, 'We had no money. I dressed in service station bathrooms, inside a door that was half-open to shield me from the crowds. Almost every location was donated, because director Fred Keller was from Buffalo, a favourite son.

'And I found that there is really a difference between television acting and film acting. Features are not where I want to go exclusively, and I don't think features are going to be there exclusively, to tell you the truth, but I like to see feature and television actors crossing over, killing that "country club" mentality. When I did this feature, I discovered that I had become a television actor. And I had to stop relying on television technique: relying on that instinct, doing those habitual things that helped me through six years of *Dallas*.'

All things considered, Patrick got more from *Vamping* than the money he didn't earn on points. 'It was a real departure, and that's healthy. I now do *Dallas* fresher. I come back to Bobby fresher. I don't know too many people who can avoid easing up on the amount of energy they put into a character, unless they can break away from it.'

In coming seasons, Patrick found other – often more lightweight – ways to break away from Bobby. He hosted a variety special for CBS called *Yearbook: Class of 1967*, in which he, singer Natalie Cole, actress Betty Thomas and football player Lyle Alzado took a nostalgic look at the sights and sounds of their high school days. More recently, he and Marie Osmond co-hosted the National Songwriter Awards in Nashville (Patrick did parts of it in a blond wig and tartan jacket!); he co-hosted the glitzy 'People's Choice Awards;' and he's done TV commercials for everything from local radio stations to seat belts to Sun Country wine cooler. Once, he even played guest-host on *The Tonight Show*, filling in for Johnny Carson.

'I just wanted to take a risk,' he said. Soon, he would take the biggest risk of his career.

10

Bobby James Ewing, 1948–1985

'I don't want to go more than four years with the show,' said Patrick Duffy about *Dallas* way back in 1979. And in 1983, he did threaten to leave the show if his character didn't change from 'boring Bobby' to something a little stronger. 'I approached Lorimar,' he said, 'and asked its head, Lee Rich, if I could get out of my contract. But the answer was no.'

In 1984, he again got restless. 'If *Dallas* ran forever,' he said at the time, 'I don't think I would stay with it. I have this year and one more year left on my contract. All things being equal, I would like to get away at the end of that period and do something else permanently. I would go right back in and do another series, but I've done just about all I can do with this character. I'm getting tired of it.'

'I never felt appreciated,' he told *TV Guide*. 'I got real frustrated with the static quality of the character I was playing,' he told *USA Today*. 'I was itchy to leave,' he told *Us* magazine.

'I had my problems with Lorimar for a couple of

years,' recalls Duffy. 'They weren't letting Bobby grow or do anything. He was really stuck, and everyone else was chewing the scenery. Absolute purity is not very interesting, as far as I'm concerned. I don't think anybody can compete with Larry's character. You can only have one character like that.'

About 25 weeks into the 1984–85 season of *Dallas*, the lead actors' contracts all came up for renegotiation. Charlene Tilton's Lucy Ewing was allowed to exit the show quietly, because her character had ceased making an audience impact. An ailing Barbara Bel Geddes, recovering from heart surgery, had been replaced by Donna Reed. The plot could always be retooled to accommodate the health, or lack thereof, of both the actors and their characters.

Patrick went to lunch with Phil Capice, Leonard Katzman and Lee Rich. He went for the express purpose of quitting. And as Patrick recalls, they looked at him and said, 'I don't suppose there's anything we can do to change your mind?'

'We tried to convince Patrick to stay,' later recalled Capice, who was now replacing *Dallas* daddy Leonard Katzman as executive producer – but that's not the way Patrick remembers it. 'They thought anybody could play Bobby,' said Patrick, just as Reed could step in for Bel Geddes, or Emma Samms for Pamela Sue Martin on the competing *Dynasty*. 'They thought we were like computer parts.'

Lorimar did offer Duffy a $10,000 a week raise over and above his $40,000 a week salary (that's not including his directorial stipends). *Star* magazine printed that Duffy's 'bid for $10,000 a month (sic) is turned down!' (On another occasion, they called it a $14,000 raise.) The *National Enquirer* said '*Dallas* Gives Bobby Ewing the Boot . . . Duffy let it be known that he wanted a raise in his whopping $70,000 per episode (sic) salary.'

The fact is, money had nothing to do with it. Patrick Duffy felt he had done all he could do with the role of Bobby Ewing, and he wanted to try new things. Against the advice of his attorneys, his friends – even his children – Duffy walked. The only person, aside from wife Carlyn and agent Joan Scott, who supported him in his decision was the local greengrocer, a leader at the Duffys' Buddhist temple. 'I didn't know if I was on the right track,' Duffy told interviewer Mary Murphy. 'He told me that a good farmer looks at a crop and knows when to pick it. It might not appear to be the right time to others, but the farmer knows best.

'That's when I quit.'

He went home and told Padraic his decision. 'Sooner or later word is going to get out,' he said to his eldest boy, 'and before someone at school says something, I want you to know I've quit *Dallas*. Padraic asked, "What new show are you going to be on?" I told him I didn't have another. And he screamed "You quit *Dallas* and you don't have another show to go to?!"'

On 3 April, 1985, the cast and crew of *Dallas* watched Patrick Duffy (or his stunt double) get mowed down by a car driven by Morgan Brittany (or her stunt double), as he heroically pushed his newly reconciled love, Pamela, out of the way of danger. Then there were at least nine retakes of the Ewing family gathered around Bobby's deathbed – retakes necessitated by the fact that real tears were streaming down the faces of cast and crew. They watched 'that little blipper ... his little heart stopped ... Bobby died,' as Patrick puts it. It was his 191st – and final, he thought – appearance as Bobby Ewing.

'I died on my last day of work,' Patrick told Tom Green between the time the show was taped and the date it aired. 'If the heartbeat machine is still going when they freeze frame, something is amiss.'

On 17 May, 60 million Americans – and 300 million others in 98 countries – watched Bobby Ewing die in a 90-minute season finale. 'I didn't want Bobby to disappear in a fiery plane crash so that he could parachute to safety as someone else,' Duffy said. 'I asked that they not just plug another actor into the role. I wanted to go out boots first, toes up – sort of like Rin Tin Tin.

'I wanted to die heroically: I didn't want any cheap shots. I didn't want one of those situations where, after I leave, my character is resurrected in some way.'

'Bobby's fans are loyal,' said Patrick. But Esther Shapiro, co-creator of *Dynasty* (who used the parachute-to-safety-as-someone-else trick in her own show) wondered, 'Is it Duffy, or Bobby that viewers love?'

That was to be the sixty-four thousand dollar (or, more accurately, $2.5 million) question.

'The show can go on as long as Larry doesn't get bored,' said actor Howard Keel, who had stepped into Jock's boots as clan patriarch Clayton Farlow.

Ken Kercheval, who plays poor Cliff Barnes, expressed little sympathy. He felt that if Bobby was boring, it was Patrick Duffy who made him so. 'That's the actor's job, to fill in the lines,' opined Kercheval. Cliff himself is an all but 'lobotomized' character, said his alter ego, but 'it's how you interpret the character that makes the difference. I'm the one who has to make him interesting.'

'The character can go as far as the actor wants to take it,' said Phil Capice, between whom and Patrick there was little love lost. 'Patrick has helped make the show a success, but it would go on quite well without him,' a 'producer connected with the show' was quoted as saying. Another 'insider source' said that 'Patrick complained so loud and long about how boring the Bobby character was, that the producer finally said "Yea, he's right. Bobby *is* boring. We're going to eliminate him."'

But those expressions of ill-will were by far the minority opinion. When actor Steve Kanaly (Ray Krebbs) came to bid his 'half brother' adieu on the set, there were saltwater tears in his eyes, not glycerine substitutes. It wasn't a parting between Ray and Bobby, Duffy said, 'but Steve and Patrick.'

Larry Hagman invited the entire Duffy family to his Malibu home, and gave Patrick first a joke gift, of course (a box of safety pins from Hagman's J.R. wardrobe, collected for the past seven years), and then a real one: a hand-engraved Colt .45 with the inscription 'To my brother Patrick, thanks for the best seven years of your life.'

'It was like losing one of the family,' said a viewer in Queens, New York. 'I hated it when he died,' said another. 'If he had to die, Pam should have died also.'

A Manhattan real estate agent actually taped the show on her VCR, in order to 'watch the last one over and over if I feel like crying.'

Would these fans warm to Dack Rambo as Jack Ewing, Southfork's new White Hat? Would they follow Pam's pregnancy with the same attention, now that the baby's father was buried? Would the return of Barbara Bel Geddes compensate for the loss of Patrick Duffy – as well as for the reported $1 million it cost to buy Donna Reed out of her contract? Would *Dallas* regain its leadership in the ratings, after falling a disheartening .1 of a Neilsen point behind *Dynasty*? (Ironically, Bobby's onscreen death pulled in three million more viewers than had watched the season cliffhanger for *Dallas*'s arch-rival glossy series, starring the woman who might have been Pamela.)

And what show would Patrick Duffy step into? Because, surely, the prime-time powers-that-be weren't going to let someone that marketable slip through their fingers.

'I went out into the cold, cruel world,' said Duffy in a national magazine, 'and nobody wanted me.' But the reporter who quoted that line in all seriousness was obviously unfamiliar with Patrick's dry sense of humour. In fact Patrick Duffy made more money outside *Dallas* than he had ever made from the show.

He immediately went into negotiations for a 'Tom Selleck-style' adventure series that he would star in. The show was optioned as a mid-season replacement, but Duffy wasn't pleased with the direction the scripts were taking, and the deal fell through at the last minute. The contract included an automatic directing clause for Patrick, and was developed under the aegis of his own production company.

He also co-developed a half-hour comedy pilot with Lorimar, centred around male and female firefighters sharing quarters in a single stationhouse. And there was talk about a *Dallas* spin-off to star Duffy and Priscilla Presley, taking the characters of Bobby and Jenna to a new location. But Patrick didn't want to keep being Bobby.

'I would only go back to being Bobby,' he said, 'if *Dallas* became a comedy and I could become Bobby's ghost, rising out of the grave to torment J.R.'

In one interview, he explained, 'I'm not one of those holdouts waiting for the absolute "right thing" to come along. I don't want *Hamlet*. I like to work; I'm a workaholic. Which is why I'm out back of my house building and digging and painting right now.'

There was one pilot series he would have given his eye-teeth for: *Cold Steel and Neon*, a cop show with a strong element of that same 'familiness' that gave *Dallas* its endurance. 'The best pilot I ever read,' Patrick calls it. 'I said "Yes, I would like to be considered for that."' But ABC preferred an actor 'who looked more streetwise,' as Duffy put it, and hired New York daytime-soap veteran Robert Desiderio (husband of *Who's The Boss* star Judith Light.) The show, retitled *Heart of the City*, aired for half of one season and folded.

Perhaps it would be a ratings-topper today if it starred you-know-who?

It was barely a week after Bobby expired that Patrick was back on a set, filming an *Alice in Wonderland* special for disaster-film producer Irwin Allen. Patrick said he originally hoped that Larry Hagman could play Tweedledum to his Tweedledee, but *Dallas* shooting schedules made that impossible. 'So I played the goat,' laughed Patrick. He also did a Home Box Office cable special with Carrie Fisher, called *From Here to Maternity*– 'a silly thing,' Duffy called it, but he enjoyed himself.

'Nobody had ever seen me crack a smile,' he says, 'so I did the "George Burns Comedy" thing,' an episode in a half-hour anthology series that ran for one season. Professor Zaslove would have been proud! All in all, Patrick did, 'acting-wise, just enough to keep the exercise going.'

The first broadcast peek that American viewers got of the new Patrick Duffy was in an episode of the series *Hotel* (which itself revamped its *Love Boat*-like format to capitalize on the success of *Dallas*-style serials.) He played a psychotic killer with three distinct personalities; 'a real departure,' Patrick called it. And he co-starred with another ex-soaper lead, Pamela Sue Martin, in the Operation Prime Time mini-series *Strong Medicine*.

'I did that one for three reasons,' he says, 'none of which was the script. One was the money, two was a chance to work with Douglas Fairbanks Jr and Dick Van Dyke, and the third was to get to take my family to London. We went on location to England for six weeks, of which I worked a little over two weeks.'

The role was something he calls 'Bobby with a stethoscope' (including an on-camera death that occurs when his character is hit by a car while trying to save his wife – 'I tried to talk the producers out of that one,' he laughs.) 'I enjoyed working with Pamela Sue Martin, but the movie . . . was fairly light in terms of any importance.'

While in Britain, he researched his family's geneology, did a series of advertisements for bedding (*very* sexy pictures) and, more importantly, started a production company in Ireland for upcoming film projects that he would produce personally. 'We closed one deal to co-produce a film in Ireland, a romantic adventure about an American writer living in Ireland.'

Unfortunately, it turned out that their Irish co-producers, the European Motion Picture Company, were an alleged front for the Irish Republican Army, and the monies raised were, reportedly, intended to buy weapons rather than film stock. The deal fell apart.

Duffy became national spokesman back home for Southwestern Bell, but none of this was of primary concern. 'Patrick was very candid about the fact that the year was devoted mainly to getting himself set financially for his family,' says an acquaintance. 'He did that with his toy company and his land company, and he is definitely a multi-millionaire today.'

'I made more money in the last 12 months than I did in any 12 months I was on *Dallas*,' Patrick said at the time.

The toy manufacturing firm, based in St. Louis, has remained so low-profile that Duffy's ownership cannot even be verified at this date. But the land development project is ongoing, it is growing, and it is hugely profitable.

'We started the project over a discussion at Patrick Duffy's house,' says Chuck Varga, owner of Western Winncor – a division of Lifescapes by Patrick Duffy & Associates. 'The company was officially incorporated within about three months.'

The firm is in land development and the construction of custom homes; its first 119 dwellings are planned for a Scottsdale, Arizona subdivision called Montaña Ranch.

'The cheapest home starts at about $595,000,' says Varga, 'and they go up to about $995,000. The architectural style is what you might call Pueblo or Santa Fe. Each one is unique, and liveability is the main concern.'

'There are very precise building codes that Duffy helped to develop,' says reporter Sam Rubin, who researched Montaña Ranch for an article that was never published. 'He's building one home there for his family, as well. It's an effort to create a perfect family environment: horses, bike trails, all that kind of thing. For the most part, they're selling empty lots – and there are only certain contractors you can use to build on them.

'Montaña Ranch is really very, very impressive.'

Patrick says that he hopes to build about eight homes each year, and make them 'fantasy houses [that are] affordable.' That is, if you call getting negligible change from $1 million 'affordable.'

'It takes a large financial commitment to build a home worth $800,000 to one million dollars,' says Varga, 'and without getting into specifics about who's put up what money, each partner feels their contribution is equal.' The other partners are contractor

David Moline and architect Shelby Wilson. Varga acts as director of marketing, and Duffy is half idea-man, half-spokesman. 'Patrick's involvement is based on the amount of time that he has available to him,' says Varga. 'A lot of ideas, we discuss over the phone. If he can't come here, we'll fly to where he is.'

Although Varga had met Duffy a few years earlier, they got involved in business dealings when 'Patrick came to Scottsdale, and researched myself as a developer and an individual. He's a very shrewd businessman; very cautious about what he gets involved in. He sought a lot of independent advice from many outside people before getting involved in anything.'

Duffy likes to think of himself as having 'hands-on involvement in the design and construction' of the houses, but Varga smiles and suggests that an actor's work schedule may cause him to underestimate a contractor's definition of 'hands-on'.

'Let's put it this way,' says Varga. 'Of all the partners, I think he's got the easiest job. We put up with the day-to-day headaches. He hasn't had quite the time and input he would like to have had. But he does have shared input . . . especially when we bug him enough.'

Patrick Duffy likes to quote James Garner in character for the classic 'Maverick' westerns ('another actor who was successful after leaving a series!'). The roguish Maverick brother used to say: 'My pappy always told me the two things you don't discuss in public are how much money you make, and women other than your wife.' But even if he won't say so, rest assured: Patrick Duffy is rich. Very rich. And for one motive: 'The security of my family is paramount.'

11

Bobby Redux

Meanwhile, back at the ranch . . .

J.R. sobs over Bobby's grave: 'I wish I'd taken time to tell you that I loved you. . . . Good-bye, Bobby. I miss you.'

J.R. isn't the only one who misses Bobby. The audience misses Bobby. They are not enthralled by plots that hinge on lesbian Greek shipping tycoons, Swiss financial cartels, Columbian emerald mines, Down's Syndrome and wardrobe battles with *The Colbys*. 'Personally, I watched the show exactly twice all year,' says Duffy.

The show had lost its sense of 'family.' 'Family in the sense of where they came from,' says Duffy, 'their shit-kicking background. They're rich, but they throw it around like the Texans do – all of a sudden, the show turned into Architectural Digest and Gentleman's Quarterly.' And one of the reasons for that change was the loss of creative control by Leonard Katzman, who had left to take the helm of another series called, fittingly, *Our Family Honor*.

With Phil Capice in Katzman's seat, a real-life feud was brewing on *Dallas*, a feud that rivalled the traditional Barnes-Ewing conflict for sheer animosity. Larry Hagman cared less for Caprice's management style and the-bold-and-the-beautiful sub-plots than did Patrick Duffy. He publicly called Caprice a 'no-talent,' and, in a manoeuvre worthy of J.R. himself, reportedly offered the producer $1 million (out of his own pocket) to take a hike.

But mostly, *Dallas* just wasn't the same without Bobby. 'You make a cake and leave one ingredient out, and it's not the same cake,' says Patrick. Series ratings fell to an all-time low; from an average first-place year-end rating, it crawled only to number six. Horror of horrors, *Dallas* failed to make the weekly top ten 'something like 15 times' during the season, says Duffy.

A survey conducted by Beta Research, Inc. in New York determined that the American viewing public considered the killing of Bobby Ewing 'the biggest prime-time blunder in TV history.' By a five-to-one margin (and with an even greater ratio among female viewers), America hollered that a Bobby-less *Dallas* was 'just plain dumb,' and insisted that he be brought back.

Fans began a write-in campaign to ask for Bobby's return; 'I'm getting more fan letters now than I was last year,' said Duffy. Patrick tied with Burt Reynolds and Sylvester Stallone in a national Sexiest Man poll – even though he was off the air. It looked like his earlier prediction that 'In a couple of years, nobody will know who Bobby Ewing is' was incorrect.

Equally off the mark, it seemed, were his predictions that 'I'm leaving Southfork permanently' and that 'I will not, under any circumstances, come back as Bobby Ewing.' When in London filming *Strong Medicine*, Patrick was beseiged with questions about a possible return to *Dallas*. He repeatedly denied that he would ever return: Not as a look-alike, not as an evil twin, not as Bobby's ghost.

But fans continued to hope. 'He may decide he doesn't like being dead,' ventured a suburban New York viewer. Duffy's reaction: 'I feel sorry for *Dallas*.'

There was plenty to feel sorry for. *Dallas* had lost its *raison d'etre*, and an average three to four million US viewers each week. In no uncertain terms, the audience had answered Esther Shapiro's question: Patrick Duffy was not an interchangeable computer part. He would not be soon forgotten. His death would not be forgiven.

It was 27 February 1986, and it was time for some fancy footwork.

'When I quit, I really quit,' says Duffy. 'I enjoyed the year, did everything I set out to do, and was ready to keep on doing it.

'Then, Larry called me. He said, "Want to come out for lunch?" Then he uttered the fatal words: "I want to talk some business." Now, I know Larry. If he wants to talk some business, he would just blab it on the phone. Something was up.'

Patrick joined Larry at a Mexican restaurant, and then the two repaired to the Hagman hot tub. 'We're sitting in my Jacuzzi,' recalls Hagman. 'I said, I don't want you to say anything to anybody about this meet-

ing, but they want you back and I want you back and
the team wants you back.

'The same afternoon, I was in a bar and a girl walks
in and says, "Gee, I just heard on the radio that you got
Patrick to come back." Someone at Lorimar had
already spilled! I laughed for days.'

'Larry said the people at Lorimar had asked him
about our relationship,' says Patrick. 'Was he still real
close to me? They said, "Why don't you talk to him
and see what his attitude is about coming back." At
lunch, I said I didn't really want to come back.

'I never thought anything would come of it, until I
got another phone call from Larry, saying "Well, they
say they're serious, and they would like to sit down
and discuss it with you." I thought, "Now we're going
to have to do some serious thinking."

'I'd never really seriously thought about it before. I
talked to my wife, and we figured whether we could
keep the production company going and I could run it
in absentia from the set. What all the particulars were.
I realized how terribly serious they were.

'Then we started talking about it.

'They told me, "You have to go back to the show.
It's not the same without you." The ratings said that,
too. Lorimar came in and said, "What will it take to get
you back?" And we told them and they said "Okay."

'If I'd known they were going to say okay so fast, I
would have started higher!'

Duffy has said that Larry's 'basic argument for my
return was money, the fun we'd have, money, the
family feeling of the cast, money, our future together,
and more money.

'I've read the insinuation that the reason I came back was because my career bottomed out after I left. I've got to talk to that guy, show him my tax return. It wasn't the money.'

Actually, the first thing Patrick asked for was the return of Leonard Katzman, whose *Our Family Honor* series had folded its tent. He got that. He asked for a continuing commitment to direct a minimum number of episodes each season. He got that.

He also asked for a million dollars. And he got that, too.

'Bonus money is nothing new in Hollywood,' said columnist Frank Swertlow. 'Producers often hand out bonuses above and beyond actors' weekly paycheques. It's a ruse . . . to keep salaries low or on a par with those of other actors in the show.'

Of course, Duffy's new salary was hardly to be low. He was raised from $40,000 a week to $75,000 a week – some estimates pegged it at between $85,000 and $100,000 a week, but Patrick doesn't talk about dollars. 'They gave me everything I asked for except the state of Idaho,' is how he put it. The deal for 32 upcoming episodes totalled out at right around two and a half million dollars in Duffy's pocket.

The *National Enquirer* trumpeted that the cost to Lorimar was 'a mind-boggling $4.2 million,' and that Duffy's deal included demands for a dressing room as big as Hagman's; partial reimbursement for an on-location residence in Dallas; Patrick's pick of any part in any Lorimar series after *Dallas* had run its course; and a promise that 'his new character will be as appealing and exciting as his old one, Bobby Ewing.'

They also printed that Carlyn Duffy burst into tears when Patrick agreed to go back, because as 'a devout Buddhist, she feels the show is too steeped in adultery and greed.' Laughs Patrick, 'We got a charge out of that one, how she was so sad because she didn't like the steamy scenes. That's the stuff she likes best!'

On 14 May 1986, syndicated television stations around the country aired *Strong Medicine*, the mini-series Patrick had done with Pamela Sue Martin. No one was paying very much attention, though; they already knew that on 16 May, Patrick Duffy was going to be back on *Dallas*. A month of anticipation made that episode the most-watched of the season.

Pamela Barnes Ewing Graison wakes up the morning after her wedding to the sound of running water. She walks to the bathroom, opens the shower door, and Bobby – 'or a man who looks exactly like Bobby' – says . . . 'Good morning.'

Victoria Principal was as surprised as anyone when she saw the episode. Because when she had filmed the show, actor John Beck was in that shower.

'That scene was a whole story in itself,' says reporter Sam Rubin. 'Duffy and Leonard Katzman went to an out-of-the-way studio in Hollywood – not the usual Lorimar studio, and not the usual Lorimar crew – and they said they were filming a television commercial. It was supposed to be a commercial for Irish Spring soap. They had all the dialogue, Patrick talking about this soap, and they filmed a complete ad spot – all to get that one line, "Good morning."'

'The media had never been so interested in Patrick

Duffy as they were when he showed up in that shower,' says Russell Turiak. And it was a virtual flood of speculation that greeted the news of Bobby's return. When CBS announced in April that Duffy was coming back, TV watchers and industry-watchers alike waited eagerly for mid-May to find out the manner of his return. Patrick Duffy was definitely back. But was beloved Bobby Ewing back?

Lorimar told the *Los Angeles Times* that 'only three people in the company' knew whether Duffy's return was even permanent, much less what form it would take. The night the fabled shower scene was aired, no one was a jot more informed. Bobby Ewing – or someone who looked just like him – had come back, and was taking a shower in Pammy's bathroom. All we knew for sure, twinkled Katzman, was 'that he will come back clean.'

The *New York Times* pared the possibilities down to these: that Bobby's eyelids fluttered on the way to the morgue; that it was a plot by J.R. to remove his brother from power; that it wasn't the real Bobby who had died the year before: Bobby had a twin brother whom even his mother didn't know about; that Mark Graison had got plastic surgery done to make him look like Pam's dear Bobby; that Pam had dreamed the whole thing. Patrick Duffy wasn't giving so much as a hint; he wouldn't even tell his mother how he was to be written in (of *course* reporters called her!)

The *New York Times* inadvertently left out the one plot possibility that became the most discussed scenario: that a Bobby imposter had undergone plastic surgery in order to weasel his way into Pam's life and the Ewing fortune. And Leonard Katzman had tons of fun with that one.

'That standard operating procedure of filming three or four alternate versions of a cliffhanger solution, so that even the actors don't know what's going on – well, they say they do it more than they actually do it,' claims an inside source. 'But when Duffy was coming back, they did shoot some fake scenes in a hospital room, with Duffy's face being unbandaged as Hagman looks at him. This was shot at Lorimar, and pictures were taken off the video screen.

'And the pictures were deliberately leaked, dropped anonymously into the murky gossip market. The *Enquirer* almost bought the pictures for $10,000 – but their field reporters in Hollywood felt sure that the pictures were faked. Instead, they were sold to the *Star*, who paid $12,000 for them and got egg all over their face!

'Lorimar was delighted about the whole thing.'

Katzman reportedly taped three complete alternate solutions to the riddle of Bobby's reappearance, at a cost of $25,000.

The *Star* ran the unbandaging photos on the cover of its 1 July 1986 issue, along with snippets of the faked scene's dialogue: 'J.R.: Oh, my God, it can't be. Why? How? . . . My God . . . How?'

People magazine ran a five-page story utilizing inside-industry clues, like contract renewals, to predict the scenario. Actress Jenilee Harrison, whose character had been bombed to bits in the last season's closer, got a telegram terminating her contract – and a

second one a few weeks later saying 'Disregard previous telegram.' This suggested a dream explanation.
John Beck had not been re-signed. This suggested that
a surgically altered Mark Graison could now be
portrayed by Patrick Duffy instead. But Steve Forrest,
who played Ben Stivers and who just might have a
hidden son strongly resembling Bobby Ewing, *had*
been re-signed – hinting at an Evil Twin scenario.

Victoria Principal was definitely fitted for a new
$2,300 wedding dress, which confirmed a second
wedding. But would she be marrying Bobby, his
benign lookalike, or his nefarious imposter? Or was
the dress, perhaps, merely a $2,300 red herring?

Patrick Duffy told the magazine, 'The parents of the
kids at my school pressure their kids to pressure my
kids to find out. I tell the boys to treat it like a present:
If we wanted you to know what was inside, we would
have wrapped it in cellophane.'

Sam Rubin knew the truth. And no one believed
him.

'It was about April or May, months before he actually came back to the show,' says Rubin. 'The
Enquirer got an anonymous phone call from a guy
deep in the bowels of the San Fernando Valley. He
said he knew how Bobby was coming back. He was
buddies with, or had fixed the car of, a CBS executive;
or his sister had served dinner to some honcho at
Lorimar; or his brother-in-law was a chauffeur –
whatever. He knew he was sitting on a hot story. I
drove out to this industrial section of North
Hollywood, and he sat me down and said, "You're not
going to believe this. It was all a dream."

'And I said "No way."'

'He insisted and insisted. I rushed to a phone booth in the middle of nowhere, and I called the office. They relayed the tip on to the boss, and he didn't believe it. No one believed it. So even though we were told the story months ahead of time, we didn't even consider printing it.

'The answer to the question all America was asking lay in a little shop in the San Fernando Valley, and we had the story. And we passed on it.'

The dream idea was dreamed up by Leonard Katzman – but he was not the only one. Carlyn Duffy also talked with Patrick about how the character of Bobby could return with all loose ends neatly tied up, how everyone could save face, and 'as soon as the audience picked their chins up off the floor,' *Dallas* could go back to square one. She said that it could all have been a bad dream.

Leonard Katzman came over to Patrick's house, and he said 'Here's how we're going to do it. It was all a bad dream.' And Patrick and Carlyn just looked at each other, and laughed.

On 26 September 1986, Pamela Ewing sat up in bed, stretched, and said to Bobby, 'When I woke up, I thought you were dead. I had a nightmare, a terrible nightmare.'

At first, the media reacted with howls of outrage. This was, after all, a 'trick ending' right out of DC Comics circa 1953. *Saturday Night Live* used pop star Madonna to parody the line. Columnist David Bianculli of the *Philadelphia Inquirer* said the twist 'ranks among the most stupid and spineless plot lines ever presented on television.' *TV Guide* dubbed it 'The Ewing Oil Shaft.' *Rolling Stone* called it 'the single dumbest show in the entire history of American television,' and captioned their picture of Bobby in the shower: 'Where Is Norman Bates Now That We Need Him?'

The audience, however, bought it. We didn't care how Bobby came back as long as *he came back*. Within weeks, *Dallas* had regained its top-ten status in the Neilsen ratings, and viewership increased by approximately four million persons a week.

'I got off a plane in L.A.,' says Patrick, 'and the first couple of people who recognized me in the baggage claim area started clapping. Then they all started clapping, welcoming me back. It really felt good.'

Patrick felt welcomed by his cast family, too. 'It was like the year really had disappeared. It was like I went to work the next day. I was back in my chair with my name on it and it was like, nothing's different. I felt not one glimmer of animosity or jealousy. In fact, I get a lot of knowing, congratulatory looks. I am treated perhaps a little differently – I am not the same person who left – but it's like an acknowledgment that I was important enough to bring back. Not more important than anybody else, but important. It was like we acknowledged Larry after the "Who Shot J.R." holdout.

'It's so difficult to say some of these things without sounding like you're tooting your own horn. . . .'

Not everyone in the cast was as supportive as Duffy likes to think. Susan Howard, whose character

Donna Krebbs had increased in importance over the previous, now-nonexistent year, was relegated again to second-string status. 'Sometimes the less said is best,' coughs Howard. 'I liked the storyline about the handicapped child. I felt we were making a contribution to society, and it was successful. I've got to completely turn around and forget that ever happened, and maybe the opportunity to do that type of work will never raise its head again on a show like this. I would have taken us in a spin-off. . . .'

'At the beginning of last year, I finally got to do what I wanted to do – to act,' says Linda Gray. 'No more victim. For me, last year was a high. When Patrick came back to "save the show", I was not happy. The show wasn't in trouble, as far as I was concerned. What kind of slap was this?'

'I'm not complaining,' says Priscilla Presley, 'but I liked it when I got to do more scenes with other people. I know that the foundation of the Ewing family was its men, and Leonard warned me that that's basically where it's going again.'

'It's nice having Patrick back,' says Steve Kanaly, 'and it's nice having Leonard back. But that was a nice storyline we had developed with Susan Howard and I, raising children late in life and the problems of the handicapped. It was nicely received. . . . One actor leaving doesn't cause the demise of any particular show. The whole prime-time line-up has changed. Thursday night is the big night on television now.'

Jenilee Harrison, whose on-screen life was saved when Bobby was resurrected, is more encouraging. 'Patrick's return can do nothing but pull us up.

Anybody who denies that is being foolish. He's come back to save the show, and that's a fact. He can do nothing but help us all keep our jobs. . . he can keep *Dallas* around.'

Says Hagman: 'It's back to the old fun and games again! It's better for me and it's better for everybody. We have the team that made it a hit back together again. Everybody's feeling good, everything's running smoothly.

'Last season was boring. Now we're putting out a better product. And even if we don't count for much in the hierarchy of earnings at Lorimar . . . little old Lorimar used to be a mom and pop operation. Now they're in the Fortune 500. [Corporate publicist Barbara] Borgliatti came up to me and said, "Hey, we're moving over to MGM, to the Thalberg Building!" I said, "What are you going to call it?" And she says, "How about the Hagman building?"'

12

Murder In Montana

'As proud as Duff was of his son,' says a friend, 'he never approved of the religious path that Patrick had taken. He thought of it as something God would punish Patrick for. And he told Patrick that.

'It makes me shiver to think that Duff would say this is how God punished Patrick for being a Buddhist: By taking his parents.'

Patrick Duffy defied his parents when he married Carlyn 14 years before, and the ice between them was only just beginning to thaw. Patrick took Carlyn and the boys to Boulder for a Montana-style hunting-and-fishing holiday at the end of the summer of '86; it was the first time he had seen his parents face-to-face in more than three years. He made plans to come back to Boulder for Thanksgiving, ready to give his children a chance to know their grandparents.

And Terrence and Marie were contemplating in earnest the possibility of moving to California; they had got as far as Vancouver, British Columbia, where they stopped to see the World's Fair while driving out

in the new motorhome that was to be their retirement-
village-on-wheels.

After 36 years, 'Duff' and 'Babe' were finally con-
sidering selling up The Lounge, the bar where Patrick
and Joanne Duffy Hunt – now a police lieutenant in
Bellvue, Washington – were raised. In July of 1986, the
senior Duffys leased the bar to prospective owners Jim
and Gayle Stubblefield, and the newcomers offered to
take it off their hands permanently. 'We wanted to buy
the place,' said Gayle Stubblefield, 'but we couldn't
reach terms – not on price, but on how we would run
his bar. He wanted the owners to run the place exactly
as he had for 30 years.'

Terrence Duffy didn't approve of the young, bois-
terous crowd that was coming to the Lounge under
the Stubblefields' management. That the place was
doing good business mattered less to him than that
loud music and loud voices were resulting from it.
Duff asked the Stubblefields to leave, and regained
ownership of the Lounge on 15 October 1986. It
reverted to being 'a place where you could bring your
wife without fear of hearing any dirty language,' as one
patron put it. The singles crowd quickly drifted back
over to The Bowling Alley tavern, leaving the often
dour Duff with his old-timers and a minion of
regulars. The rowdy 'cattleman's bar' that Patrick
Duffy remembered from his youth – a place where 'my
dad has thrown as many people out of that bar as you
could count ... and has been hauled away in an
ambulance' – had long since mellowed with age.

The back building abutting the Lounge had always
been the Duffys' homey kitchen and bedroom, and the

bar itself was more or less their living room. The carpet was red, the wallpaper red and gold, and the tables black with wooden chairs. They had decorated it themselves. Behind the 25-foot-long bar were photographs of Patrick as Bobby Ewing, and of the two tavern television sets, one was invariably tuned to *Dallas* on Friday nights. Since Duff usually worked the late shift, Babe would generally tape the show for him.

They were proud of their son; they just didn't let on.

'People aren't star-crazy up here,' says Steve Devitt, former editor and publisher of the regional newspaper *Montana Maverick*. 'Celebrity isn't something folks would make a big deal over.

Patrick Duffy didn't spend much time up here. Everyone knew his folks, but few knew him. I don't even recall seeing his pictures in the Duffys' bar – and I've been to the bar, because the hub of activity for any journalist is the corner bar.

'It was a nice bar, a quiet bar. Myself, I tended to patronize the bar across the street.'

'When Patrick Duffy came to Boulder, the townfolk never acknowledged him as a big deal,' discovered veteran newsman Tony Brenna. 'They expected him to fit right back into their plaid-shirt slot: "So he made it big in show business; so what?" But once he got on a plane and departed for *Hollywood*, they were all intensely proud of him, and said so.'

Chubby-cheeked, blond-haired Kenneth Miller was like the majority of the area's residents: The Montana native had no idea that 'Bobby Ewing' had grown up in the next town, and probably wouldn't have given much of a damn if he had known. He was a 19-year-old janitor from Helena, 28 miles along the highway from Boulder, and he was never going to be rich or famous or live in Hollywood.

The girl he had taken to his high school prom labelled Kenny 'real nice,' and 'popular at school.' Born and raised in Helena, Miller's childhood was a distorted reflection of Patrick's own all-American boyhood. Kenneth liked to fish and hunt – but he enjoyed it even more when the fishing and hunting was legally out of season. He hung tight with his homeboy buddies, playing games of dare and double-dare – and racked up a juvenile misdemeanor record for his escapades. He never had much money – which is why he and his friends bought beer by the keg, and grass by the joint.

'He didn't have much of a career, but there's not much career opportunity in this area,' said an observer. 'You can't help but feel sorry for young people in that area; there's nothing there to do.'

To Patrick Duffy, that was a motivation. To Kenneth Miller, it was an excuse.

Miller's buddy at the Kleen King janitorial service had managed to get himself out of the sticks, out to fabled California, leaving behind a series of unhappy foster homes and a future that promised . . . nothing. Sean Wentz, also 19, succeeded only in earning a California arrest warrant for car theft, and hitchhiked to Montana in the spring of 1986.

The tall, bearded Wentz seemed worldly-wise and exotic to baby-faced Miller. Miller's new buddy was even going steady with a 24-year-old divorcee, the mother of two children. Tamela 'Tammy' Harding thought the world of Sean: They talked of a future together. They would kick their drug habits together, they would finish their haphazard therapy sessions together, they would get married and live happily ever after. Even Tammy's father, Kingman 'Butch' Harding, a former sheriff's deputy, was optimistic about Sean's potential for rehabilitation.

So when the two boys met on Tuesday morning, 18 November 1986 for a day out together, no one worried. Miller told his landlord he was off for a day of rabbit hunting, and took his shotgun. The landlord didn't cock an eyebrow. That such a day would conclude with a hearty pub-crawl was par for the course. In Patrick Duffy's suburban Los Angeles neighbourhood, two teenagers carrying shotguns and six-packs of beer are a walking felony; in Boulder, they're just part of the scenery. 'We have a lot of guns in Montana,' says area native Steve Devitt. 'We don't have a lot of armed robberies.'

Accounts of the events that unfolded during the evening of 18 November differ, even the eyewitness accounts – and especially the accounts of Miller and Wentz themselves. But this much is certain: The young men, dressed in regulation jeans, work-shirts and windbreakers, came into the Lounge sometime after 7 p.m. There was one customer in the bar, nursing a 75-cent beer, who believes it was right about 9 o'clock. Wentz, trying to impress his more naïve buddy, flashed a twenty-dollar bill and ordered for both of them: two shots of tequila.

Wentz spoke briefly to the tall, grey-haired man behind the bar. Drinks are a lot more expensive in Californa, he said when he paid the tab, showing off his worldliness. He asked for directions to Boulder Hot Springs, a spa outside of town. Duff obliged. Miller wondered aloud if the local resort was a good place to meet girls; Duff thought not. The youngsters wandered off.

The sole customer left the bar, as he remembers it, right around 9:45. The next customers to enter were two shift workers leaving duty at the Montana Developmental Center, an institution for the mentally disabled which provides employment to much of Boulder. One parked the car, the other walked in the Lounge front door. It was just past 10 p.m. Terrence and Marie Duffy were dead.

Some witness reports said that Terrence Duffy had turned away the two young men when they first walked in; they were, after all, the kind of patrons who were his pet peeve. Some say he cursed at them. We'll never know for certain which final recollection is more accurate: the one that had Duff washing glasses while Babe worked a crossword puzzle; the one of Duff playing the tavern slot machine while Babe was off in another room; the one that placed Terrence Duffy's body slumped over the bar, or the one that left him sprawled bloodily on the floor.

Sometime between 9:45 and 10:15, when the normally quiet Lounge was completely empty, Sean Wentz and Kenneth Miller, by this time thoroughly drunk, had returned. And this time they returned with Miller's 12-gauge shotgun. They left with $97 from the till, a bottle of whisky from the back bar, and blood on their hands.

What was the fatal instigation? Did the teenagers demand liquor, and Duff order them brusquely from the premises? Did they demand the contents of the cash register,and drew weapons when Duff refused? Did they enter barrel-first, confronting bold Duff's headlong rush to wrestle away the gun? We'll never know for certain which convicted murderer actually pulled the trigger. All we know, with terrible finality, is that Terrence and Marie were blasted with two loads of buckshot and killed instantly, and that the last thing they saw was the bar they loved too much to leave.

Their killers' reaction was immediate: Both threw up when they saw what they had done. Next came panic. Miller and Wentz fled from Boulder in a stolen Volkswagen, speeding all 30 miles to Tammy Harding's house. Wentz blurted out an admission of guilt, expecting sanctuary in the apartment he and his lover shared. Instead, Tammy ordered the blood-spattered pair out of the house, and phoned her father for advice. Butch Harding called the cops.

Wentz and Miller drove their hot car to the nearby Prospector Chevrolet dealership, where Kleen King had a janitorial service contract. Wentz broke into a pick-up truck, leaving Miller to flee in the VW. The criminals left a shotgun shell and a bottle of whisky from the Lounge on the car lot grounds – which were swept up and discarded by their acquaintances on the cleaning crew, who were afraid of losing their jobs. The janitors were later charged with obstructing justice.

The boys split up, hit the twisting, icy highway – and

Wentz headed right back for Tammy's house. It was just past 11 p.m. Tammy was in the livingroom, making a police report to Detective Brad Hampton. As the stolen pick-up skidded to a halt next to the squad car, three things happened at once: Tammy screamed, Sean screeched into a U-turn, and Det. Hampton grabbed for the radio.

Seven mobile units, comprising the Helena police department and the Lewis and Clark County sheriff's office, took up the chase; by 11:30, Wentz had pulled his truck to the side of the road and surrendered. Hands above his head, he yelled at the officers 'Don't shoot!', and assumed the position against the bonnet of the truck.

Moments later, Wentz saw his partner in crime drive that unmistakable white Volkswagen right past the scene. Miller had taken a wrong turn.

'He did it! He did it!' cried Wentz, pointing to the blundering fugitive. Within minutes, both were under arrest. Each accused the other of having pulled the trigger.

The 12-gauge was still lying on the floor of the Volkswagen. Broken glass from the shattered bar mirror was sticking to the suspects' clothing. A bartender's pouring spout was rolling in the dirt.

And blood-spattered dollar bills from the Duffys' cash drawer were blowing like dead leaves in the cold November wind.

Sean Wentz and Kenneth Miller were each charged with two counts of deliberate homicide. They had no idea who they had killed.

'There was never the slightest indication that this

happened because these people were Patrick Duffy's parents,' says Steve Devitt. 'It happened because this was a bar, a quiet bar, and it looked like an easy hit. It happened because two kids were drunk and wanted some cash. As a crime, it was depressingly standard. They were stupid, they were drunk, they said, "Don't leave any witnesses."'

The last major crime Devitt can remember in this sleepy community is a case of second-degree murder – 'a drunk beat his wife to death' – some ten years ago. 'The biggest news story I covered in Boulder,' says Devitt, 'was the time they changed the garbage-collection regulations, and assessed everybody a ten-dollar tax. The courthouse was packed.'

A robbery-murder in Boulder was big news locally. KTHZ-TV news director Ian Marquand received a sheriff's report about the tragedy at his Helena office in the middle of the same night, but 'there didn't seem much point in going all the way out to Boulder at that hour. We coordinated efforts to cover the scene the following morning.'

When it came time to notify the Duffys' next of kin, however, everything changed. The police telephoned Joanne. Joanne telephoned Patrick. Someone telephoned the wire services. And then all hell broke loose.

13

Media Gone Mad

'I was fast asleep when the phone rang,' says senior *National Enquirer* reporter Tony Brenna. 'I had just returned from Japan; I was exhausted. It was the middle of the night, early in the morning – all I remember is the total shock of being awakened with a call from the head office that Patrick Duffy's parents had just been murdered. Even as I was rushing to Burbank airport, I couldn't assimilate it. All the stories I'd worked on about this guy: Here he's so massively successful, has this million-dollar salary increase, happy family, everything a man could dream of. And, *wham!* Some voice on the phone says "Go to Montana; Patrick Duffy's parents have just been murdered."

'I never really thought of him as being from Montana.

'There were no direct flights, naturally, so I changed in Salt Lake City. There was already another reporter on the plane. So was Duffy's sister, but no one recognized her. We landed between mountain peaks at this tiny little airport with one long runway. There's maybe three flights a day out of there. When I stepped off the plane, there were already camera crews on the tarmac.

'Duffy's sister walked right past them.

'It was an incredible scene. There was press from Britain, from Germany, from France, even from Japan. Television men with camera crews, newspaper report-ers – between the soundmen and the photographers and everything else, there must have been 150 arrivals already. The *Enquirer* alone sent six reporters, four photographers, and hired four stringers locally. Ord-ers to block-book hotel rooms were coming in from around the world; I saw colleagues I hadn't seen in years, people I last saw on Fleet Street in London, or in New York at the United Nations.

'The first place they all went was Hertz Rent-A-Car, and snapped up every four-wheel drive vehicle in the county. They all thought they were in the wild, wild West. They came with snow gear, hiking equipment – they looked like they were going to the Yukon. The locals had a laugh over that. Turned out, there wasn't any snow and all you needed was your family car. They had rented all these 4-wheel drives and there was no necessity for them – luckily for me, because when I got to Hertz they were sold out.'

'We were immediately deluged with requests for footage from around the country,' says regional broadcaster Marquand. 'We were trying to coordinate information flow from New York to L.A., and cover the arraignment of the suspects at the same time. Was there cooperation among the media? No, I wouldn't call it cooperation. I would say we were requested to cooperate with other people. We got nothing in return.

'I know that if you're from a major urban centre and you come to Montana to cover an event like this, you're not going to handle the story in the same way the local media would. They wanted juicy details about the killings, pictures of the bodies, pictures of the suspects, pictures of Patrick.

'We never expected sensitivity from them. But we have to live with these people, make our careers here. Granted this event is not one you can be proud of, but the town was certainly not shown in its best light. Local residents felt . . . violated.'

'I'd guess the press corps reached 300 altogether,' says Devitt, himself called in to assist a national weekly. 'That's a lot of intrusion for a town this size. Most of them were working for the tabs, and a large number of them were British — which is another thing you don't usually see here: foreigners.

'By and large, even the *Enquirer* did a very solid job of covering the story. The problem was, they were looking for something beyond what was really here. For all the media blitz, this was a very straightforward news story. The celebrity element was absolute coincidence.'

Representatives of major news media like the Associated Press or the *Los Angeles Times* did.. t have a particularly tough assignment, although an unexpected (and all but unprecedented, in this kind of crime) judicial gag order did keep much of the legal information closed to them. Basic legwork was sufficient to complete their articles: the manner of arrest, cause of death, amount of bail, pleas of innocence and shifting of blame, the chronology of events. Facts have a comendable tendency to consistency; they sit still and wait for you to find them. The same cannot be said for emotions.

The celebrity press, for whom this was a Story of the Decade, needed more than the amount of bail ($250,000 each, quickly raised to $500,000 each) or the detention facility (Lewis and Clark County Jail, later transferred to Jefferson County Jail.) Their readers already knew – or didn't care – whether the car-chase took 21 minutes or 35; whether Miller drove the VW or the pick-up truck; whether Wentz resisted arrest. They cared about how this was affecting their dear 'Bobby'. They wanted to share his pain.

No one can blame Patrick Duffy for declining to expose his pain to the world. He had every reason and every right to close the door on the media. But 300 million people were begging for a story, and 300 reporters were being paid to give them one. If they couldn't go through the front door, they'd slip in the back.

The hordes descended on The Lounge, which had been roped off by law enforcement. So they peeked in the windows. They camped on neighbours' porches. Photographers perched in trees, set up tripods on the forecourt. While *People* magazine sequestered Tammy Harding and her father, competitors bearded Tammy's neighbour in the apartment house laundry room. Brenna and Devitt tracked down Kenneth Miller's landlords, employers and schoolmates.

Patrick was whisked in on a Lorimar company jet, and disappeared from view. 'Mr Duffy has no statement at this time,' said a Lorimar spokesman. Deadlines were approaching.

'We had been there 24 hours, working all night,' remembers Benna, 'and our copy had to be filed within 12 hours. Everywhere we went, there would suddenly appear another reporter, waving a chequebook. I don't think there was a single friend, relative or neighbour who had ever had any contact with Patrick Duffy since his childhood that wasn't contacted by the press.'

'Everyone was trying to get Vern Sutherlin, who runs the Boulder *Monitor*,' says Devitt. 'He was a friend of the Duffys. I managed to speak with his wife.' (Others resorted to his son.) 'I heard he sold some photographs for $5,000 or $10,000 – and that's a hell of a lot of money in Montana. Cost of living's cheap up here.'

A bounty went out on any piece of artwork that an editorial department could wrap a story around. 'They were paying $1000 for a picture of Duffy when he was a kid,' frowns Brenna. 'More if he was with a dog. The locals went from impressed by all this attention, to upset and offended by it, to figuring out that it meant free food and drink for the whole town. Everyone had their hand out. The editor of a local paper was on the payroll of about four different operations. Reporters were paying people to show them Duffy's favourite swimming hole, or the spot [where] he caught his first fish – and *other* reporters were paying people to spy on *them!* It was a bizarre media spectacle.'

Brenna and Devitt, beat reporters at heart, dutifully stationed themselves in Helena and investigated. They got names, addresses, dates, background data – but what they needed was heartache, shock, agony, friendship and irony. They needed the collective emotion of Boulder, Montana. And the communal memory of Boulder was raped.

'The townspeople reacted in three camps,' says Devitt. 'Some were angry that the media would only show up for something like this. Some were amused, bemused, and a bit bewildered by it all. And there were those who wanted a moment in the spotlight, who wanted to tell their story.'

Merely by virtue of their Boulder address, 'residents themselves were becoming overnight celebrities,' says one writer. 'National media fought with overseas media for interviews with barflys. Free booze was flowing like tapwater. It stopped having anything to do with Patrick Duffy, much less his parents. There was never a tangible sense of his presence. If he had come forward, I don't think it all would have gotten so insane. The writers couldn't get to Duffy, so they grabbed for anything, from anyone. They were desperate.'

'One of the problems with this kind of information-gathering,' notes Devitt, 'is that you usually end up interviewing someone in a bar after buying him his fourth round. There was a great tendency – and incentive – to make a good story a lot better. A number of residents blew Duffy's involvement with Boulder way out of proportion. One guy said that every time Duffy came to town, he'd visit the local high school. I went out there, talked to the students – turned out he had been there once, briefly. There were a lot of stories about how he would tend bar for his dad every time he was in town – also untrue, as far as I could tell.'

It would be funny if it weren't so sad. Published reports look like a kindergarten game of 'Telephone Operator.'

The London *Sun* reported that Sean Wertz was apprehended on Tammy Harding's front stairs. The paper printed that Larry Hagman had said of the Duffys, 'I knew them better than I knew Patrick' – because he had once posed for a photograph with them during a Montana vacation. They said Patrick and Carlyn were at a mountain temple, chanting for his parents' reincarnation.

People magazine chose to focus on Sean Wentz, having secured an exclusive interview with his fiancée. This relieved much of the burden of finding out facts regarding the actual story. Better to reveal that Wentz was a heavy metal addict, and name the Metallica cut that he 'listened [to] continually through earphones: "Kill 'Em All."' The few statistics they did print were off, though not by much.

USA Today made a point of mentioning that the presiding judge the accused would face 'is no stranger to the public eye. [Frank] Davis was judge at the 1985 trial of two self-styled mountain men who kidnapped a world-class athlete to make her a wilderness bride.' This incident eventually became the subject of a made-for-TV movie, by the way.

Even the estimable *Time* magazine incorrectly reported that Patrick had 'left the former mining camp after high school to find fame on the top-rated soap.'

The *Globe* story led with the 'scoop' that Terrence and Marie were expecting Patrick three days hence, and that he was planning to move them into 'an extension to his house [built] especially for them.' They described the robbery as having netted $30, called Patrick and his parents 'extremely close,' and attested that Terrence had never once seen a single fight in his bar.

The *News of the World* – a safe distance across the Atlantic – missed every single fact. But not by enough to warrant a libel suit. The Duffys had owned the bar 'for over 40 years.' They were 'tidying up . . . when two baby-faced gunmen burst through the door and demanded the night's takings.' Their bodies were discovered 'hours later.' The paper quoted speeches of pain and regret that Patrick never made. As background filler, they mentioned that Patrick abstains from alcohol, lives in a 30-room mansion, and drives a Mercedes.

Depending on what publication you consulted, Patrick was informed of the tragedy by Leonard Katzman/Joanne Duffy Hunt, right after it occurred/ early the next morning, and immediately/after lengthy consideration informed his children. As quickly as possible/after 24 solid hours of chanting to Buddha, Patrick and Carlyn/Patrick alone flew to Boulder/ Helena and drove with friends/was driven by police to the scene. They/he stayed with friends in town/at a mountain retreat some miles away.

The only point on which they all agreed was this: Patrick Duffy cried.

14

Aftermath

Patrick Duffy reacted to the news of his parents' deaths with shock and horror. He was stunned, he was confused and he was amazed. But not once did he cry.

Duffy flew to Helena in the Lorimar company jet on Wednesday afternoon, 19 November. A police car took him to the home of friends in Boulder, where he joined Joanne and locked the doors behind them. They said nothing to the media.

The first public statement regarding the crime was made by producer Leonard Katzman, who said that 'everyone on *Dallas* and at Lorimar TV is shocked and devastated ... overcome with grief.' This was Wednesday morning, and the *Dallas* set was shut down as a token of mourning and respect. Later that afternoon, Lorimar spokesperson Barbara Brogliatti released a prepared statement explaining that Patrick had telephoned the cast and crew to request that they continue work as usual.

On Wednesday afternoon, Lorimar spokesperson

Bob Crutchfield read a prepared statement from Patrick on the steps of the Boulder post office: 'To those who have voiced their concern, I want to thank them for their love and for understanding my family's need for privacy at this time.'

On Thursday, a representative of the sheriff's office read a second statement from Patrick: 'I never fully appreciated the loyalty and depth of concern my fans all over the world had for me and the character I portray.'

In the four days Patrick stayed at Boulder, he was glimpsed a total of four times: Getting off the plane, entering the Lounge to pick up a few of his parents' effects, driving to the home of friends for dinner, and entering the Lounge to collect some bottles of liquor.

Terrence and Marie's bodies had been sent to Missoula for an autopsy, as is mandated in cases of death by homicide, and Joanne called a mortuary in Bozeman, 100 miles away, to arrange for their cremation. She stated that her parents had specifically asked for cremation rather than burial, and wished that there be no memorial service. In lieu of flowers, the senior Duffys had requested donations in their name to the Boulder Ambulance Service.

Mortuary proprietor Eldon Dahl reported that the cremation took place on Thursday, 20 November. The ashes remained in an urn at the mortuary until Joanne Hunt could be contacted back in Washington; then they were forwarded to her home near Seattle.

No member of the immediate family ever set foot in the funeral home.

'He's a cold son of a bitch, that one,' said one

newspaper editor covering the story. And out of his
desire to respect his parents' privacy, to 'keep the
press from turning this into a circus,' in the words of
the mortician, Patrick appeared to some as having no
respect for those same people – no love, no warmth.

'I read so many accounts of me breaking down and
crying,' Duffy told TV interviewer Barbara Walters in
his first public discussion of the tragedy, three months
later. 'I don't know where they got them. So far, there
hasn't been a fall-down weeping moment about it.'

Every tabloid account of Duffy's reaction to the
news of the murders described him in tears. Without
an eyewitness, they all printed what they presumed to
be true. Everyone expected him to cry.

What he did was to chant. 'The first thing Patrick
did,' said a fellow member of his NSA chapter, 'was to
sit down and chant for the people who had murdered
his parents. His parents have only moved on to
another life. Killing their bodies didn't take their
souls. For years, Patrick has been chanting for the
karma of his family – and in our practice, we believe
you can affect the karma of seven generations to
come.

'But the people who killed his parents, they will
create an effect as great as the cause they committed.
No one escapes the universal law of cause and effect.
Patrick doesn't need vengeance; he knows those boys
will have to face their karma.

'Patrick sent a message back to the group, the whole
NSA organization, and we chanted for him. He
chanted 24 hours for his parents, to insure that their
souls go to a good place. He knows that if he wants to

see them again, he can just chant about them.'

In these terms, Patrick sounds more loving and warm. He also sounds like a space cadet – which is why he avoids using this kind of language. But when you try to put these concepts into non-Buddhist terms, a great deal gets lost in the translation. Patrick gives logical definitions of karma; he usually describes it as 'total responsibility for what happens to you.' When you apply that to a double homicide, it sounds dangerously close to 'They had no one to blame but themselves.'

Staying in his L.A. shrine room for almost a day rather than rushing headlong to his parents' home come across as self-indulgent, even callous – unless you, too, embrace the Buddhist concept of chanting and have faith in its power. Patrick Duffy knows quite well that his actions can seem 'cold and unfeeling' to non-believers.

Non-believers like Terrence and Marie.

The Lounge was boarded up, the Duffy kin left Boulder, and the press wandered away. Kenneth Miller and Sean Wentz stayed behind bars; Steve Devitt returned to Missoula. 'They will be tried, and Duffy won't be at their trial, and the link will be broken. There will be no more front page coverage,' he predicted. He was right.

Knowing in his soul that cosmic justice was assured for his parents' murderers, Patrick Duffy felt no need to oversee their earthly punishment. Both boys pleaded not guilty at the 3 December arraignment; each blamed the other. The arraignment earned two short paragraphs in the newspapers. Kenneth Miller stood trial for two counts of homicide, robbery and assault on 9 March at the Jefferson County courthouse. He testified that he had been an unwilling accomplice. The trial was covered in seven paragraphs.

Miller was convicted on 19 March and sentenced to 180 years in prison: 75 years for the murder of Terrence Duffy, 75 years for the murder of Marie Duffy, 20 years for robbery and 10 years for assault – to be served consecutively. Three column inches ran in the Sunday *Los Angeles Times*.

Patrick Duffy did not attend any of the proceedings.

On 6 May 1987, Sean Wertz reversed himself and pleaded guilty to two counts of deliberate homicide, presumably in a bargain to avoid the death sentence. He is expecting the same 180-year sentence.

Both convicted killers continue to deny responsibility for the crime, each insisting that the other was the triggerman.

Patrick Duffy has made no public statement regarding the sentence. He demanded no vengeance, expressed no satisfaction. Sean Wentz said: 'If someone killed my parents, I'd want them dead.' Patrick said he just wants 'a type of world out there where this doesn't happen to anybody.'

15

Down Home At Home

If his fans found it difficult to understand Patrick Duffy's reactions to his parents' death, that's not surprising: People often have trouble understanding Patrick Duffy altogether. He may be 80 per cent Bobby Ewing, but the 20 per cent that differs, differs enormously.

'Patrick is not all Bobby,' said Victoria Principal. 'He is a much more complex man.' She spoke with a reporter who had been trailing Duffy for more than a day, and commented, 'If you followed him around for six weeks, you could not do a thorough investigation.'

Principal, despite the fact that the two have conducted a long-term and often highly public sniping session with one another, has nothing but on-the-record admiration for her co-star. She calls him 'very professional, unusually bright, and aware of his craft at all times.' Larry Hagman, of course, considers him a true brother. Steve Kanaly calls him 'a fun guy with a great deal of leadership – although he is something of a rascal.'

'He's very friendly with the crew,' says reporter Sam Rubin, who has interviewed most of them at one time or another. 'They regard him as very likeable and very unaffected. He come across as warm and funny and nice.'

Lili Ungar, who worked with Duffy on *Vamping*, calls him 'a rare breed. Charming, easy-going – doesn't take himself too seriously. A real professional; one of the most pleasant people I've ever worked with.' Construction company partner Chuck Varga says 'I consider him a very shrewd businessman. He doesn't jump into things without a lot of forethought, and doesn't rely strictly on his own opinion but seeks independent advice – which is a sign of a good business person.'

Photographer Russell Turiak remembers him as 'nice, friendly, cooperative, professional. Easy to deal with. Very down-to-earth.' Rock band booking agent Rick Bloom, who helped organize a SAG benefit for then-union official Duffy at the Hollywood Bowl, says 'he's just about the *realest* human being of any actor I've known.' Journalist David Houston, who spent many hours with Patrick and a tape recorder, had only one caveat after the bull-session: He said it's a shame that the actor's roles are so straight-laced. 'Patrick has a wonderfully dry sense of humor,' wrote Houston. If you've seen Duffy sparkle on television talk shows, you'd revise 'dry sense of humour' up to 'downright hilarious.'

Even the housekeeper he fired refers to him as 'a real doll.' Never is heard a discouraging word about this man – although we did find one acquaintance of another *Dallas* star who thinks Patrick is 'egotistical and arrogant, one of those jumped-up-truckdriver actors.' He must not have known about all that classical and Shakespearean training.

Patrick's wife, who knows him better than anyone in the world, calls him 'the most charming man I have ever met. The nicest, kindest man you could possibly find, incapable of doing a nasty deed. . . . Patrick is sensitive, practical, funny, spontaneous and clever. He has all the good elements of a child's personality, but that quality is tempered by his maturity.'

Another woman's point of view – that of actress Deborah Presley, who has appeared on a number of 'Dallas' episodes – might give Carlyn pause, if she didn't know her husband so well. 'All I can say about Patrick,' laughs Presley, 'is that he's a huge flirt. I remember the first time I worked with him; we had a scene together in a hospital corridor. I had never met this man before in my life – I didn't even recognize him – and he came up to me, hooked his arms around me, and waltzed me away down the hallway. I wriggled out of his grasp, said, "Who are you, and where are we going?" and he just laughed and laughed.'

'Patrick freely acknowledges the fact that he is an admirer of all women, and he relates to them on a very comfortable level,' writes Patrick's long-term agent Joan Scott in Duffy's own press biography. 'I love women. All shapes and sizes,' said Patrick. 'I am probably attracted to more women than any man has a right to be, whether he is married or not.'

But, outside of that admitted indiscretion almost 15 years ago, Duffy has held fast to the old song-lyric

admonition: 'You can look, but you better not touch.'
'I'm wired to a receiver on my wife's wedding ring,' he
joked with talk-show host Phil Donahue, 'and she picks
up this little hum when my heart rate gets too high!'

Patrick and Carlyn Duffy are wired together, but by a
spiritual connection rather than an electrical one.
Their bond is almost mystical. 'Once, we decided to
get our boys something instead of toys,' he told *Us*
magazine. 'We went shopping separately, and both
came back with the same edition of the works of
Shakespeare. That's the reality of being in perfect
rhythm with each other.'

Patrick says that the only opinions he really values
are Carlyn's and his own, 'and I'll listen to her over
me' anytime. The two still hold hands in public. He
keeps pictures of Carlyn and their sons, Connor (7) and
Padraic (11), in his Lorimar studios dressing room,
and tries to pick up the boys from school himself when
he's not on location. The family works around the
house together, plays together, and often crawls into
the big master bed together. He's devoted to his boys,
and proud as punch of them.

He says he tries to be a disciplinarian with the
children for their own good, but usually ends up as
'the biggest soft touch I know.' He often sees himself
aping his own father's treatment of himself as a child,
and it brings him up short. 'Sometimes when I do or
say something, I think back to the time and place
when my father acted exactly the same way. Then I
say, "God, that's my dad. There he is again,"' and he
shakes his head.

'I'm very family oriented,' says Patrick. 'Home life first, family life first.' He doesn't like the glare of the media intruding on his nest, although he never fails to mention is sons and give shared career credit to Carlyn every time he opens his mouth. 'I don't like all that attention focussed on my family,' he says. Sometimes, the combination of his acknowledging Carlyn's equal partnership in his life together with his reluctance to put her centre stage speaking her own piece, leads to headlines like 'Wife Has Patrick Duffy Under A Spell.' An article that quoted a former employee as believing 'she treats him like a puppet; Patrick is subservient to Carlyn.'

The age difference is also a contributing factor in these negative perspectives, but Patrick dismisses the decade between them as a factor against their enduring love. 'I hate this idea in Hollywood that everyone has to try to look 16 until they drop. Wives improve with age!' He even requested that Bobby Ewing be allowed to develop a few grey hairs over the coming seasons, and begged for a chance to be called *Robert*, or even Bob.

'It's like Little Joe on *Bonanaza*,' Duffy said on 'The Tonight Show.' 'I'm sure that after about year 14 he was going, "Can't it just be *Joe*?" I can't see myself 20 years from now . . . with a "Y" at the end of my name.' 'Like Johnny?' quipped the show's host, silver-haired Johnny Carson, grimacing. Peals of laughter ensued.

Patrick likes to laugh. He spent most of last season cracking 'Bobby's ghost' jokes on the set, and has been known to spend his pocket money to arrange an embarrassing set-up for Larry or Victoria – suitable for inclusion in the annual out-takes reel shown at the cast Christmas party. 'When he was co-hosting a TV special on the opening of Michael Jackson's *Captain Eo* movie at Disneyland,' recalls *LA Times* correspondent Craig Modderno, 'he brought a video camera of his own with him. He was making a birthday present for his sister, and went up to people in the crowd – not just celebrities, but regular folks, too – and had them give birthday greetings on the tape. He was having a blast.'

.He's a man of rather simple tastes,' says Sam Rubin. In fact, one of the things Patrick finds hardest to accept about his Bobby Ewing character is Bobby's free-spending attitude. 'Once, Bobby had to give away a million and a half dollars to sort out some family feud,' he said. 'I find it hard to imagine that amount – let alone give it away.'

Deep down, he's still the starving actor he was when he and Carlyn shared that roach-infested apartment in Manhattan. 'My family and I never had any money until just a couple of years ago,' he stated in an article describing the success of then-two-seasons-old *Dallas*. 'That makes everything we have a real adventure for us. When we mow our own lawn, clean our own pool, it's a ball because we never had any of those things before.'

The kidney-shaped pool isn't visible from the residential street in the West Valley town where the family has lived since 1978 in a 3,300 square foot single-storey home. It's a street of upper-middle-class working families, comfortable but in no way spectacular. The house has a wine cellar and a custom-built altar room – but it was hobbyist carpenter Patrick who helped custom-build them. From the outside, the home appears very ordinary.

Duffy's 1980 Jeep and a 1984 Dodge owned by his land development company are parked outside, as is the dingy Datsun belonging to the family's secretary. The housekeeper lives in. Neighbours seldom see the family members, calling them unintrusive and fond of their privacy. The postman likes them. Patrick happily leaves autographs pinned to the wall of a tiny sushi parlor he frequents, a few blocks away on busy Ventura Boulevard.

'He's a real down-to-earth guy,' says Turiak. 'He doesn't need fancy, show-off stuff. Last time I came to shoot him, he was wearing a camouflage jacket, T-shirt, plain jeans and boots.' Almost every magazine interviewer has described him in a similar outfit. As Patrick likes to say, 'I've dressed this way all my life. I just wear a better class of boots now.'

There are indulgences. He and Carlyn raise and show three-gaited and five-gaited American Saddlebreed horses – but they also go to the city zoo. He collects antique toys – and lets the kids play with them. He doesn't own fancy cars, but he likes them: On one *Dallas* shoot, he sped away from the set in a prop Testorossa, raced around the block three times, and returned saying 'Wow! I've never driven a Ferrari before!' For a while, he and Carlyn developed a taste for caviar, and treated themselves to purchases by the pound.

But when it comes to everyday eating, Patrick Duffy's tastes are definitely in the junk-food-junkie category. 'When he's on the set,' says Priscilla Presley, 'he eats tons of Danish and washes it all down with coffee. There's baskets of apples and oranges and cheese trays, but he goes straight for the junk food.' On one airplane trip, he passed over the first-class dinner service and instead cadged a bag of Doritos corn crisps from the flight attendant, 'and pigged out on that.' He works out in his home gym about three times a week, mainly to keep the producers off his back – or belly, as the case may be.

A man of enormous energy, Patrick seldom gets more than five hours sleep a night (although he tries to catch naps on the weekends), and is generally awake before 5 a.m. for his morning ritual of chanting. 'I would say that 364 days of the year, I am irritatingly up and happy,' he said. He credits his energy and ebullience to Nishiren Shoshu, and he wastes few opportunities to extol its virtues. 'He'd start to tell me all about it,' recalls one colleague, 'and I'd say "Patrick, enough already! I'm Jewish, I'm perfectly happy with my own religion!"'

Patrick Duffy is also perfectly happy. 'I'm one lucky son of a gun,' he told writer David Wallace, and although the fame and the fortune and all the other goals he dreamed of – and achieved – are part of that happiness, he insists that 'when I say I was just as happy driving a truck for $3 an hour as I am right now, people don't believe me. But it's true.'

16

Looking Ahead

What does the future hold for Patrick Duffy? Come to think of it, what does the future hold for Bobby Ewing?

As *Dallas* gears up for its tenth season. Bobby will once more be Pam-less, as Victoria Principal finished the previous year engulfed in flames after a head-on car collision. The actress just wrapped a made-for-TV-movie called *The Mistress*, and swears she won't come back to the show under any circumstances. 'Am I going to return in the shower?' She smiles and says, 'I wouldn't dream of it!'

Of course, we've heard that once before. And it's common knowledge in Hollywood that Lorimar still had ongoing negotiations with Principal as late as summer 1987.

'For the first few episodes,' says – to borrow a phrase from the tabloids – an inside source, 'the Pam character will be physically there but she won't be played by anyone. She'll be completely wrapped in bandages. What the producers are doing is monitoring how badly Victoria is missed. They don't want to make the same mistake twice. If they feel people want "'Pam" more than they want Victoria, she'll be unbandaged with a new face. Otherwise, she'll quietly fade away.' Press leaks hint that Lorimar has already set the stage for Pam and Victoria to exit gracefully and together; a plot twist early in the season has Pam fleeing her hospital bed, leaving behind a tearful farewell-forever note to her husband. 'Better I go now, while you and Christopher can still remember me as I was,' the horribly scarred former beauty is expected to write. By November, she will have instituted divorce proceedings.

Bobby is unlikely to bounce back to Jenna, as Jenna is being written into the arms of Ray Krebbs. Wedding costumes have been ordered, and are likely to grace the airwaves around January 1988. A new character named Lisa Alden, played by young blonde actress Amy Stock, has been signed for at least half the season, and has already shot one show that puts her in Bobby's arms. Whether she gets to stay there past Sweeps Week is debatable . . . but she definitely isn't staying as the next Mrs. Bobby Ewing. Scriptwriters have already painted her into a Bad Girl corner, making her the sister of adopted son Christopher's natural father, and determined to gain custody.

Whatever the identity of his bedmate, it's certain that Bobby will be the central character of the show for a while. Audience reaction proved beyond a shadow of a doubt that he is the single most beloved element of the programme, and that as much as they love to hate J.R., fans need his vinegar tempered by little brother's honey. Dramatic monologues galore will give Duffy a chance to emote his arse off.

Patrick will be around for at least two seasons to come – and there's an option for a third, if the show keeps going strong. Lately, prime-time soaps have lost their stranglehold on the network line-up, and industry prognosticators expect the series to gasp its last by the time Duffy's contract runs out. Then again, it could end up outlasting *Gunsmoke*. Who knows? And this time, says Patrick, he's expecting to hang in there until the final curtain.

What then? Is there life after *Dallas*?

'Duffy is, after all, ten and twenty years younger than most of the other series' stars,' says our insider. 'He could easily spin off into another show. There has already been one concept discussed that would be entitled simply *Bobby James Ewing*, moving the character and his family to a new town and building from there.'

'When my contract runs out, I'll be 40 years old,' says Patrick. 'I'll still be healthy. I can suck in the old stomach and try one more time.' Don't expect the next series to be a sprawling carbon of the earlier show. 'The next thing I enter into, I will try to make more of a one-person show, or a two-person show.'

Patrick once dreamed of starring in a Tarzan adventure, and wants to get in some Errol Flynn-style roles before it's too late: 'I must do my swashbuckling before I get out of my prime and have to do drawing-room comedies!' At the same time, however, he anticipates with relish a day when he can grow nobly into character roles, trading on his acting skills instead of his leading-man looks. 'I'd love to have someone write for me a very good piece of theatre for television, something like *Love Among the Ruins*, which starred Laurence Olivier and Katherine Hepburn,' he once said.

He wants to continue to produce, and especially to direct. But he has no burning ambition to conquer the big screen.

'I don't want to be a movie star,' he says. 'I want to do television. The pace and pressure of television is where I'm most comfortable.' There are some changes he would like to make in the nature of television *per se*, though: 'Television should be *more* explicit. Less so in sex than in violence, only because there are few people capable of depicting sex in what I think is its proper light. Fictional violence, however, is a wonderful thing, a release . . . even when done badly.'

Some mornings, Patrick wakes up thinking, 'I don't want to be acting all my life.' Other days, he thinks, 'I'm fortunate to be in a business that can last until your dying day.' But whether he moves sideways in the career arena, or chooses to stretch in his chosen speciality, he will still never make his profession the main priority of his existence.

'I'm a workaholic. Acting is my work, working is fun. I do it because I like it. But acting is not the prime motivational force in my life.'

What is the prime motivational force? His family. In that, he and Bobby have perhaps the most in common. Family above all. That, and making some small impact on the world, hoping to leave it somehow a better place by virtue of his having been in it. If his lifetime

goals are still too amorphous to define, Patrick Duffy
knows that he and Carlyn want one thing for certain:
'By the time I die, we will have accomplished everything I want to do.'

Whatever it may be.

Index